SKI TOURS
in the
SIERRA NEVADA

Volume 1
Lake Tahoe

By Marcus Libkind

Bittersweet Publishing Company
Livermore, California

Cover design by Mac Smith.

Typography by Vera Allen Composition.

Front cover photograph by Marcus Libkind: Lake Tahoe.

Rear cover photograph by Lee Griffith.

All other photographs by author unless noted otherwise.

Acknowledgement: Over the years many people have been the source of invaluable information. They include National Forest Service, National Park Service and State Park personnel, the owners and operators of nordic centers and mountain shops, friends, and acquaintances. I am especially indebted to Brian Klimkowsky for his review of the manuscript and his thoughtful comments and ideas. Above all, I must thank Clara Yen for the many hours she spent editing the manuscript.

Library of Congress Catalog Card Number: 84-73452
International Standard Book Number: 0-931255-00-7

Published by Bittersweet Publishing Company
P.O. Box 1211, Livermore, California 94550

Printed in the United States of America

To

my mother

for always being there

when I need her

and

in memory

of

my father

who would have enjoyed this moment

as much as I

Contents

SOUTH TAHOE

ECHO SUMMIT

Introduction

The guidebook series, *Ski Tours in the Sierra Nevada*, forms a comprehensive collection of ski tours which I have encountered during more than a decade of exploring the Sierra. They range geographically from the Lake Tahoe region in the north to Sequoia National Park in the south. The Lake Tahoe, Carson Pass, Bear Valley, Pinecrest, Yosemite, Huntington and Shaver Lakes, Kings Canyon and Sequoia areas are all covered in depth.

Whether you are a novice or an old timer, this series of guidebooks will introduce you to new and interesting areas which offer excellent ski touring opportunities. The information in these volumes will be useful for planning tours of an appropriate difficulty so you can enjoy more pleasurable and safer touring.

The 78 tours in this volume cover a large geographical area and are divided as follows:

> DONNER-TRUCKEE—Tours originating from or near Highway 80 except those from Highway 89 south of Highway 80, and from Highway 267.

> NORTH TAHOE—Tours originating from or near Highway 89 south of Highway 80 and north of Meeks Creek, Highway 28 west of Incline Village, and Highways 267 and 431.

> SOUTH TAHOE—Tours originating from or near Highway 89 south of Meeks Creek and north of Luther Pass, Highway 50 north of Meyers, and Highway 28 south of Incline Village.

> ECHO SUMMIT—Tours originating from or near Highway 50 west of Meyers.

I sincerely hope that the tours in these guidebooks will inspire you to explore new areas. I have thoroughly enjoyed the time spent in researching these books and I will be rewarded each time I meet another ski tourer who has found this information useful. As I would like to hear from you, let me know your comments and suggestions.

Marcus Libkind
P.O. Box 1211
Livermore, California 94550

Author's Note

There are certain inherent dangers associated with wilderness travel in winter. No guidebook can diminish the hazards nor be a guarantee of safety. If you choose to experience the mountains in winter, you voluntarily do so knowing there are hazards.

Although the tour descriptions make reference to specific, obvious dangers, you should not assume that they are the only ones. Even the safest tour can become dangerous should you encounter poor weather, or adverse snow or avalanche conditions.

Some tours may take you through private property which is not marked. If you encounter marked private property, I hope that you will respect the property rights of others so that the good reputation of ski tourers will be preserved. Similarly, some tours pass through downhill ski resorts. For safety and to promote continued goodwill it is important to stay off the groomed slopes when ascending.

Although great care has gone into researching the tours in this guidebook, you may find inconsistencies due to factors such as new construction of roads and housing, policies toward plowing roads, changes in parking restrictions, and changes in trail markers. Also, extreme variations in snowfall can make a remarkable difference in how things appear. Be prepared to cope with these discrepancies should they arise.

In the final analysis, you must be responsible for executing your own safe trip.

Backcountry solitude

How To Use This Book

The short time it takes you to read this section will increase the usefulness of this guidebook. Each tour description in this guidebook contains a summary and a narrative. The summary box gives you at a glance the significant characteristics of the tour. The narrative is a description of the route.

Below is an explanation of each characteristic in the summary box.

Difficulty: The difficulty ratings are based on four criteria: length, elevation change, steepness, and navigation. A 5 level scale for rating the overall difficulty of the tours is used. The skills associated with each level are:

1—Beginner

- Little or no previous ski touring experience
- Follow simple directions without map or compass

2—Advancing beginner

- Proficiency in the basic techniques: diagonal stride, sidestep, kick turn, step turn, snowplow and snowplow turn
- Control speed on gradual downhills
- Negotiate short moderately steep terrain
- Follow simple directions in conjunction with a map

3—Intermediate

- Excellent proficiency in all the basic techniques plus the traverse and herringbone on moderately steep terrain
- Negotiate long moderately steep and short steep terrain
- Good stamina
- Navigate using a topographic map
- Use a compass to determine general orientation

4—Advancing intermediate

- Excellent proficiency in all ski touring techniques
- Negotiate long steep terrain including densely wooded areas
- Strong skier
- Navigate using a topographic map and compass

5—Expert

- Excellent all around ski tourer and mountain person
- Negotiate very steep terrain
- Exceptional endurance
- Navigate using a topographic map and compass

Two tours may be assigned the same rating but vary greatly in the skills required. For example, a tour on a road which is long and a tour which is short but requires navigation by map and compass may both be rated 3. For this reason the difficulty ratings should only be used as a general guide for selecting a tour of appropriate difficulty. Check the summary box for information regarding length, elevation and navigation to determine whether your abilities match the demands of a tour. Also, refer to the narrative which describes the tour route for special considerations.

The tours were rated assuming ideal snow conditions. Deep powder will make the traveling slower and more difficult. Ice, sometimes referred to as "Sierra cement," will make all tours much more difficult. If you are faced with icy conditions you might consider waiting until early afternoon to begin when hopefully the snow will have thawed.

Length: The length is an estimate of the horizontal mileage as obtained from the topographic maps. Several of the tours are in meadows which are adjacent to plowed roads and in these cases the length is simply stated as "short." Also noted is whether the distance is one-way or round trip.

Elevation: The first number is the elevation at the starting point of the tour in feet above sea level. The elevation is a major consideration when planning tours early or late in the season.

The elevation at the starting point is followed by a slash and the elevation change for the entire tour. The change is written as " + gain, − loss." "Nil" is used where the change is negligible.

Navigation: The navigational difficulty of each tour is based on untracked snow and good visibility. The key words and phrases are:

Adjacent to plowed road—Tour is located almost completely within sight of a plowed road.

Road—Tour follows snow-covered roads. Although roads are normally easy to follow, a small road or a road in open terrain may be difficult to locate or follow.

Marked trail—Tour follows marked trail; may require basic map-reading skills. Markers are normally brightly colored pieces of metal attached well above the snow level to trees or strips of brightly colored ribbon attached to tree branches close to the trail. Blazes which mark summer trails are not considered markers since they are often obscured by snow. In nearly all cases, when on a marked trail you must pay careful attention to locating each successive marker which may not be ideally placed. Even with a marked trail, you will probably need some knowledge of the route and basic map-reading skills to follow it.

Map—Tour requires the ability to read a topographic map since the tour follows well-defined terrain such as creeks, valleys, and ridges. Also remember that poor visibility can make route-finding impossible without a compass and expert knowledge of its use.

Compass—Tour requires the use of a compass in conjunction with a topographic map. In some instances the compass is mainly for safety but other routes require you to follow compass bearings.

Descending from Snow Mountain

Time: To give you a general idea of the length of time required to complete a tour, I have used the following key words and phrases:

- Short
- Few hours
- Half day
- Most of a day
- Full day
- Very long day
- One very long day or two days

Some of the factors which will affect your trip time include snow and weather conditions, your skiing ability and physical strength, characteristics of the tour, and your personal habits. Consideration has been given to reasonable rests and route finding in making the estimates.

Always keep in mind that the mid-winter months are filled with short days. Very long tours are best done in early spring when the days are longer.

Season: The season is the period in an average snowfall year during which the snow conditions for the tour are acceptable. Early and late in the season the conditions may be less than optimum. Exceptionally early or late snowfall as well as heavy snowfall, extend the season. On the other hand, during drought years the season may be shortened.

A well-deserved break

USGS topo: Listed are the United States Geological Survey topographic maps, both scale and name, which cover the tour route. Parts of these maps are reproduced in this guidebook, and the map reproduction number and its page location are at the beginning of each tour adjacent to the tour name. Be aware that some of these maps have been reduced.

For a majority of the tours only the 15′ series maps are listed. The 7.5′ series are also listed if they have significant benefit. When the elevations given for peaks are different on the two map series, the elevations stated in the text are from the map series reproduced in this book.

Topographic Map Legend

●	Starting point
▲	Destination
5	Landmark number (corresponds to narrative)
▬▬▬	Highway or plowed road
▬ ▬	Ski route

If you desire to purchase maps by mail you can obtain price and ordering information by contacting:

United States Geological Survey
Box 25286 Denver Federal Building
Denver, Colorado 80225

Start and end: Described are detailed directions for locating the starting and ending points of the tour. The ending point is omitted if the tour route returns to where it began.

Keep in mind that it may not be legal to park at these points. Increased usage and recent heavy snowfalls have resulted in greater restrictions and stricter enforcement. Sometimes carrying a snow shovel will allow you to clear a place to park. At other times you may have to resort to paying for parking or walking some distance. In the near future, the California "Sno-Park" bill should provide some relief from this situation.

The remainder of each tour description is in narrative form and describes the route. Keep in mind that the description is not a substitute for knowledge, skill and common sense. For your convenience, when a reference is made to the directions given in a different tour, the name of the tour is followed by the number, e.g. "Big Meadow tour (no. 57)." Also, significant landmarks mentioned in the text are followed by a number in parentheses which corresponds to the same number found on the map, e.g. "From here descend to a road junction **(4)**."

Exploring a new route

Donner-Truckee

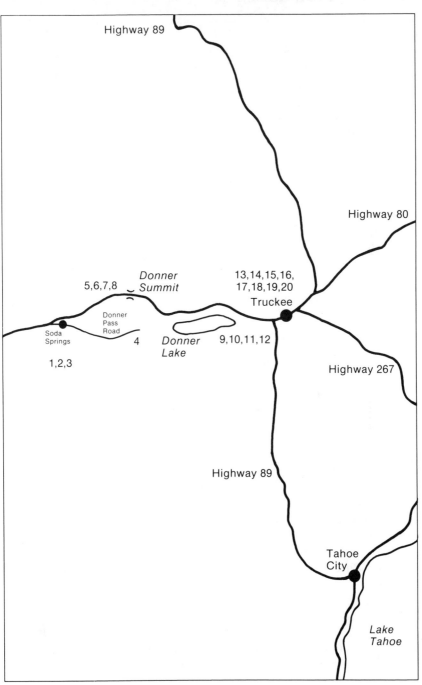

Highway 89

Highway 80

Donner Summit

5,6,7,8

13,14,15,16, 17,18,19,20

Truckee

Donner Pass Road

Soda Springs

4

Donner Lake

9,10,11,12

1,2,3

Highway 267

Highway 89

Tahoe City

Lake Tahoe

1 Cascade Lakes

MAP 1
PAGE 21

Difficulty	2
Length	Up to 8 miles round trip
Elevation	7000/Up to +700, −700
Navigation	Road
Time	Half to most of a day
Season	December through April
USGS topo	15' series, Donner Pass
Start	End of Pahatsi Road. From Soda Springs drive 0.9 mile south on Soda Springs Road. Turn right onto Pahatsi Road and continue for 0.4 mile until it comes to a dead end at the entrance to Royal Gorge Cross Country Ski Resort. The tour begins here. Parking is available on nearby roads. Be sure to follow the posted parking regulations.

Cascade Lakes are located on a plateau among many other lakes in the rolling terrain of the Donner Summit area. From the Kidd Lake vicinity on the road to the lakes, you have fine views to the north. During most of the tour, you can use the vertical rock faces of Devils Peak as a landmark. If you are a very strong skier who desires a challenging tour in this area, consider the outstanding tour to Snow Mountain which is described separately.

This perfect cross-country skiing area is also the location of the Royal Gorge Cross Country Ski Resort which charges for the use of their groomed trails on the land they own or lease. Fortunately, you can use Pahatsi Road, a designated Public Travel Way, for access to this area. The National Forest Service in Truckee can supply detailed information regarding the location of public and private lands in this area.

You begin the tour from Pahatsi Road by skiing west along the unplowed road. Ski a short distance and cross a groomed trail. Continue west and encounter another groomed trail onto which you turn left and ski for 25 yards. Turn right off the groomed trail and continue west on the road which is marked with Public Travel Way signs until you intersect a Sno-Cat track. Turn left onto the track and follow the signs. In places where the road and the Sno-Cat track or groomed trail cross or coincide are confusing, carefully follow the signs which mark the public access road.

When you encounter a sign across the road which indicates the entrance to the Royal Gorge Lodge area (1), you are 2.2 miles from the starting point. Do not follow the Sno-Cat track which leads to the privately owned lodge at Kilborn Lake. Instead continue west on the public access road until you reach the dam (2) at the north end of Kidd Lake.

From the dam, follow the road for 1.3 miles as it continues around Kidd Lake, past a second dam, over a small hill, and finally down to the dam between upper and lower Cascade Lakes. Most of Cascade Lakes and Long Lake are on public lands.

Devils Peak

2 Snow Mountain

MAP 1
PAGE 21

Difficulty	5
Length	20 miles round trip
Elevation	7000/+2400, −2400
Navigation	Road, map and compass
Time	One very long day or two days
Season	December through April
USGS topo	15′ series, Donner Pass, Granite Chief
Start	End of Pahatsi Road. From Soda Springs drive 0.9 mile south on Soda Springs Road. Turn right onto Pahatsi Road and continue for 0.4 mile until it comes to a dead end at the entrance to Royal Gorge Cross Country Ski Resort. The tour begins here. Parking is available on nearby roads. Be sure to follow the posted parking regulations.

The tour to the summit of Snow Mountain offers perfect cross-country skiing terrain and spectacular scenery. The final four miles ascends gradually along ridges and makes the return descent a cross-country skier's dream come true.

Once you are at the Snow Mountain summit, the "Royal Gorge" of the North Fork of the American River is 4000′ below you to the southeast. This grand view is only one in a spectacular panorama which includes the high peaks to the north, east and south, and the Central Valley and foothills to the west.

The difficulty of this tour to Snow Mountain is entirely due to the distance. An extremely early start, excellent snow conditions, and a long, fair weather, spring day are required to complete the route in a single day.

Your first objective is to reach the dam between upper and lower Cascade Lakes (3). Refer to the Cascade Lakes tour (no. 1) for directions. From the dam, ski south by picking a fairly direct route to the west side of Devils Peak. As you pass the peak, pick up the road which continues due south. If you see a fork in the road, follow the east (left) fork as it climbs gradually through some trees to a small ridge (4).

From the ridge, continue on the road to the east for 0.2 mile until you turn south with it. Just ahead where the road ends, continue to ski south, climbing gradually and making a course for the saddle to the north of Peak 7287 (5).

From the saddle, ski to the southwest along the ridge. Cross Peak 7287 and the next high point, and descend to the next saddle (6). Ascend south and then southwest along the northeast ridge of Snow Mountain to the main ridge. Snow Mountain is at the southeast end of the main ridge.

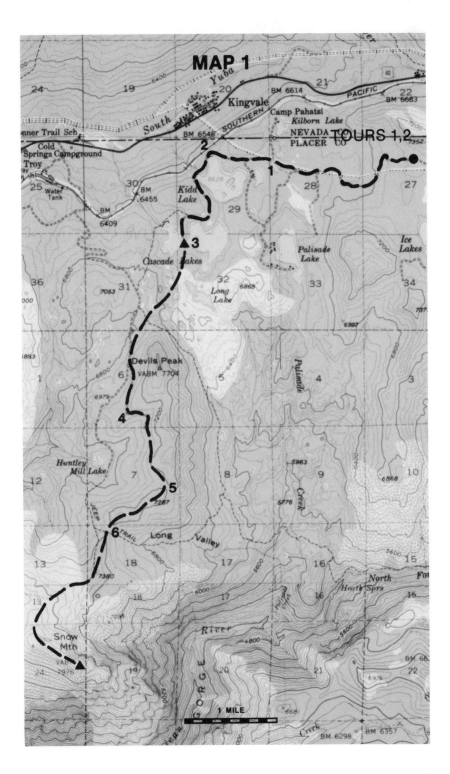

3 The Cedars

MAP 2
PAGE 23

Difficulty	2−3
Length	Up to 11 miles round trip
Elevation	6850/Up to +1350, −1350
Navigation	Road
Time	Half to full day
Season	Late December through March
USGS topo	15′ series, Donner Pass
Start	End of Soda Springs Road, 2.3 miles south of Soda Springs. Follow the posted parking regulations; do not park in the plowed area at the very end of the road.

If you pick a clear day with good snow conditions for this tour, you will be treated to an outstanding combination of good touring and spectacular scenery. This tour traverses steep canyon walls as it gradually but continuously descends more than 1000′ down a road to the headwaters of the North Fork of the American River. Since there are excellent places to stop along the route, you can shorten the tour without missing the beauty of the area.

Because this tour follows a narrow road with a steady gradient, save it for a time when the snow is soft, such as immediately after a light snowfall. Exercise caution after heavy snowfalls or during other unstable conditions due to possible avalanches along the route.

From the starting point, ski south on the snow-covered road for 1.3 miles until you cross a small ridge (1). The elevation loss of this first section which parallels Serena Creek is less than 100′. Expect the gradient to be much steeper on the remaining descent.

From the ridge, continue on the road which descends for 0.7 mile to a sharp left turn (2). Just off the road to the south is a large, open, flat area which is an excellent alternative destination. If you plan to ski farther, ski out to the rim overlooking the North Fork of the American River anyway. Snow Mountain, the ascent of which is described separately in this guidebook, is prominent to the west with its steep cliffs descending down to the "Royal Gorge." To the east, Mt. Lincoln, Anderson Peak and Tinker Knob form the ridge along which the Sugar Bowl to Squaw Valley tour traverses.

To continue on this tour, return to and descend on the road as it zig-zags down to the bridge at Onion Creek (3) which is also a good destination point. To continue, follow the road for 1.6 miles as it climbs 150′ and descends to a road junction (4).

Take the south (right) fork and ski for 0.3 mile through the summer community of The Cedars to Cedar Creek.

3

Since there is no bridge across Cedar Creek, it may be dangerous to cross. If you can cross it, you can continue another 0.3 mile, always taking the right forks where there are choices, to the bridge across the North Fork of the American River.

Once you are down in the canyon, the thought of having to climb out may seem unappealing. Fortunately, if the conditions are good on your descent, there will be a nice track to ascend on the return. Also, the gradient is steady but never excessive.

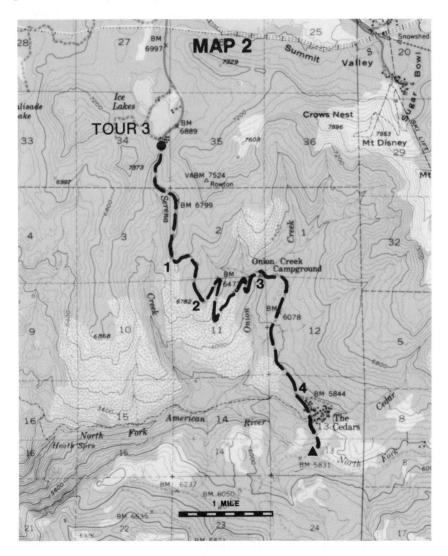

4 Sugar Bowl to Squaw Valley

MAP 3
PAGES 26–27

Difficulty	5
Length	12 miles one-way
Elevation	7050/+2000, −2850
Navigation	Map and compass
Time	Very long day
Season	Late January through early April
USGS topo	15' series, Donner Pass, Granite Chief, Tahoe
Start	Donner Ski Ranch, 3.8 miles east of Highway 80 on Donner Pass Road.
End	Squaw Valley Ski Area, 5.4 miles north of Tahoe City on Highway 89.

The tour from Sugar Bowl to Squaw Valley is a classic in the North Tahoe area. A large elevation gain and loss, traverses along windswept and corniced ridges, potentially poor snow conditions, and considerable navigation all contribute to the challenge of this tour. This tour should only be attempted during periods of good weather.

At Donner Ski Ranch, you have an excellent view of the route to the summit of Mt. Lincoln which is 1300' above. From Donner Pass Road, walk south to the train snowshed and cross the railroad tracks. Now ski south for 100 yards until you reach a snow-covered road. Cross the road, climb over a small hill, descend to Lake Mary, and then ski to the south end of the lake (1).

From Lake Mary, traverse and climb south for 1.4 miles to the northeast ridge of Mt. Lincoln (2). Then climb southwest on the ridge for 0.5 mile to Mt. Lincoln (3). As you approach Mt. Lincoln, do not attempt to ski the east bowl of the mountain because the avalanche danger is extreme.

The next part of the tour is a spectacular traverse of the high ridge between Mt. Lincoln and Anderson Peak. From Mt. Lincoln, ski southeast along the ridge for 2.5 miles to the saddle north of Anderson Peak (4). When you descend from Mt. Lincoln, make sure that no downhill skiers follow you. Also, be aware that this section of ridge is often heavily corniced on its northeast side.

From the saddle, ski a very short distance south to Benson Hut in the timber. You can make reservations for use of this Sierra Club hut by contacting:

Clair Tappaan Lodge
P.O. Box 36
Norden, California 95724

4

From Benson Hut, ski around the west side of Anderson Peak and climb up to the ridge **(5)** between Anderson Peak and Tinker Knob. Ski southeast for 1.1 miles along the ridge to the east side of Tinker Knob **(6)**.

From Tinker Knob, continue south and descend 500′; be careful not to lose too much elevation. After descending, leave the drainage you have been following and traverse south, below and to the west of a ridge until you reach Mountain Meadow Lake **(7)** which is 2.1 miles from Tinker Knob.

From Mountain Meadow Lake, ski 0.2 mile south to a broad saddle where you can see Squaw Valley below. From the saddle, descend to the southeast to Squaw Creek and Shirley Canyon. Be careful to stay clear of any avalanche paths to the south of the creek. Once you are in Shirley Canyon, follow it to Squaw Valley. The distance from the saddle to Squaw Valley is 2.5 miles.

Carving turns   *Charlene Grandfield*

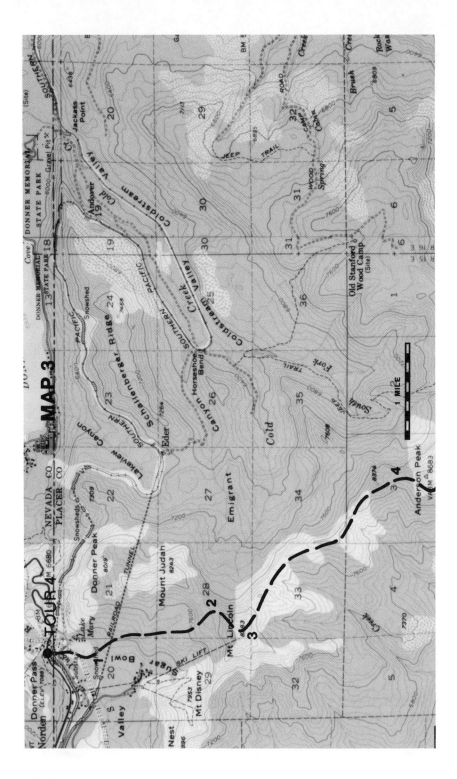

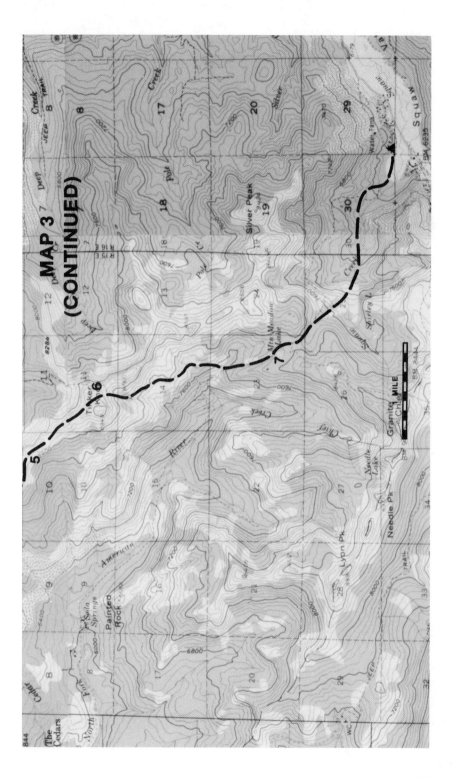

MAP 3
(CONTINUED)

27

Benson Hut   *Kim Grandfield*

MAP 4
PAGE 30

Round Valley and Peter Grubb Hut 5

Difficulty	3
Length	5 miles round trip
Elevation	7200/ + 800, − 800
Navigation	Road and map
Time	Half day
Season	December through April
USGS topo	15′ series, Donner Pass
Start	At the plowed loading zone on the north side of Highway 80 at the Castle Peak Area and Boreal Ridge exit. Parking is available at the east end of the frontage road which is on the south side of the highway.

Peter Grubb Hut, built by the Sierra Club in the thirties, is a popular destination for ski tourers. Located in Round Valley, the hut is used to make the 5.2 mile round trip tour into an overnight trip. To use this Sierra Club hut, make reservations well in advance by contacting:

Clair Tappaan Lodge
P.O. Box 36
Norden, California 95724

Begin the tour by skiing 0.1 mile east on a road which parallels the highway. Follow the road as it turns northwest for 0.5 mile until you reach the edge of the meadow in Castle Valley.

With Andesite Ridge to your west (left), climb steadily on the road for 1.2 miles to the northwest. The climb ends with a short steep section which leads to Castle Pass (1).

From Castle Pass, ski north for 0.6 mile and traverse the west ridge of Castle Peak. Finally, descend for 0.2 mile into Round Valley where Peter Grubb Hut is located. Round Valley is formed by Castle and Basin Peaks.

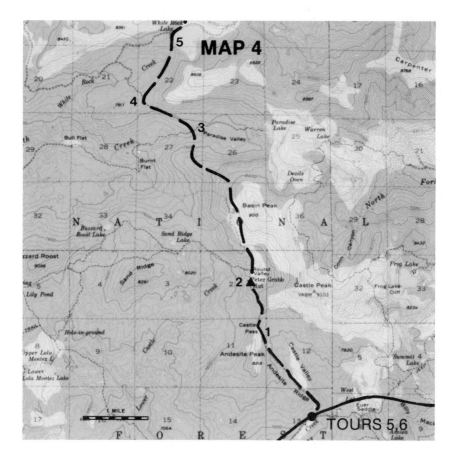

MAP 4

TOURS 5,6

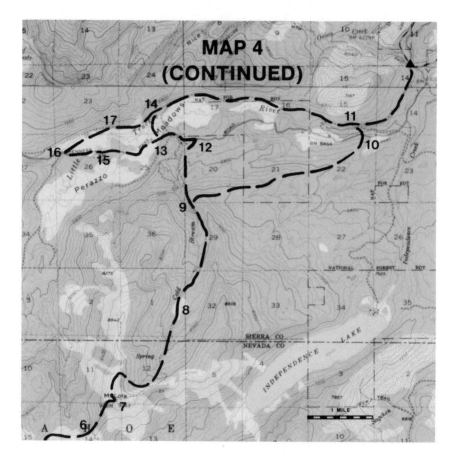

MAP 4
(CONTINUED)

MAP 4
PAGES 30–31

6 Boreal Ridge to Highway 89 via Mt. Lola

Difficulty	5
Length	18 to 23 miles one-way
Elevation	7200/ + 3000, − 3800
Navigation	Road, map and compass
Time	One very long day or two days
Season	Late December through early April
USGS topo	15′ series, Donner Pass, Sierraville
Start	At the plowed loading zone on the north side of Highway 80 at the Castle Peak Area and Boreal Ridge exit. Parking is available at the east end of the frontage road which is on the south side of the highway.
End	Junction of Henness Pass-Jackson Meadows Road and Highway 89, 15 miles north of Highway 80.

Don't miss this tour if you have the skills and stamina to do it. This tour covers a multitude of terrain as it weaves from Castle Valley to Round Valley to Paradise Valley and then climaxes with the ascent of Mt. Lola which commands a spectacular setting. Once on the summit, you still have an exciting 2700′ descent along Cold Stream to the Little Truckee River.

As you can imagine, once you leave Round Valley and Peter Grubb Hut behind, you find yourself quite alone. Since the length and the route-finding are challenging, only very competent backcountry travelers should attempt this tour.

You can ski this tour in a single day when the days are long and the snow is well-consolidated, such as in early spring. If you intend to do this tour earlier, such as in the winter, expect to spend a night or two snowcamping.

Begin this tour by skiing 2.6 miles to Peter Grubb Hut (2) as described in the Round Valley and Peter Grubb Hut tour (no. 5). In this section, you ski through Castle Valley, cross Castle Pass, and descend into Round Valley. Since you need a very early start for this tour, you are likely to miss the crowds which often journey to the hut.

Your next goal is Paradise Valley which is 2.5 miles from Round Valley. From Peter Grubb Hut, climb and pass Basin Peak to its west. As you pass Basin Peak, Paradise Valley is directly to the north on the far side of a steep cliff. Shortly after entering the trees, turn northwest and descend along a shoulder of Basin Peak. Once the terrain to the north looks moderate, turn north and drop down into Paradise Valley (3).

Paradise Valley is wooded but not dense enough to obscure the view to the northwest where the route heads. Traverse and climb to the northwest for 0.9 mile to the saddle (4) between Peaks 7911 and 8606.

From the saddle, ski northeast for 1.0 mile to White Rock Lake (5). If you descend to White Rock Creek, which you may have a tendency to do, you must climb up to the lake. You can avoid this climb by traversing along the base of Peak 8606 until you reach the lake.

Ahead of you now is the big climb to the summit of Mt. Lola, 1350' in 1.9 miles. From the north side of White Rock Lake, ascend to a saddle between two unnamed peaks and then follow the ridge east to one of them (6). In this section, be aware of small but potentially dangerous cornices.

From the peak, continue northeast along a narrow ridge for 0.6 mile and then turn east and climb at a very steep angle to the summit of Mt. Lola (7). If you are doing the tour in a single day, don't get too cocky once on the summit since you have only covered 8.8 miles at this point. Nevertheless, take time to enjoy the outstanding view.

The next challenge is to drop down to Cold Stream which you follow north. Be wary of dropping directly from the Mt. Lola summit into the drainage as there may be a cornice to the northeast. A good route off the summit is to ski north along the ridge of which Mt. Lola is a part. At an appropriate point (there is no landmark), drop down to the east and follow the drainage as it turns into Cold Stream.

Ski north along Cold Stream and enjoy the easy but fast terrain. When you reach a meadow (8), continue along Cold Stream for another 1.5 miles until the drainage narrows and descends abruptly (9). At this point,

Frozen lake

6

you must make a choice which determines the total length of the tour.

Shortest route. To follow the shortest route, climb east from Cold Stream. If you began climbing at the correct location, you find yourself on a ridge which descends gradually to the east and slightly north. Ski down this ridge for 2.8 miles to Henness Pass Road (the old road from Highway 89) **(10)**. From the road, ski north for 0.2 mile until you reach the Little Truckee River which you must ford. There used to be a bridge here which was used to reach Independence Lake, but it was washed out years ago, and there are no plans to rebuild. If you choose this route or the "medium route," you would be wise to carry a spare set of socks and a small towel for the ford.

Once on the north side of the river, follow the road for 0.2 mile to Henness Pass-Jackson Meadows Road **(11)**. Turn east (right) onto and follow it for 1.5 miles to the east and then northeast to the end of the tour. Via this route the total length of the tour is 18 miles.

Medium route. Continue from the point **(9)** where Cold Stream narrows and descends abruptly by skiing north and descending along its east side. You must pick your way through trees as you descend at a very steep angle for 0.3 mile until the steepness lessens. Continue north until you intersect the Henness Pass Road **(12)** which you intersect just to the east of the cabins shown on the topo.

From the cabins, ski west on Henness Pass Road for 0.4 mile until the terrain opens up **(13)**. At this point, you must make another decision. You can save 2.5 miles by skiing north for 0.2 mile to the Little Truckee River. Since there is no bridge there, you must ford the river. This ford is easier than the one on the "shortest route" because you can usually find a shallow spot at which to cross. If you want to avoid the ford, see "longest route."

Once across the Little Truckee River, ski north for 0.2 mile to Henness Pass-Jackson Meadows Road **(14)**. Follow the road east (right) for 4.5 miles to the end of the tour. This route is 20 miles long.

Longest route. The longest route is for those who do not want to ford the Little Truckee River. From the point where the terrain opens up along Henness Pass Road **(13)**, continue southwest for 0.6 mile through the open area in the direction of the road until the road enters the trees. Enter the trees and follow the road west for 0.4 mile to the Little Truckee River **(15)** where there is a bridge.

Once you are across the bridge, continue skiing west on the road for 0.5 mile until you reach a junction **(16)**. At the junction, turn northeast and ascend along a road for 0.8 mile to Henness Pass-Jackson Meadows Road **(17)**. Here turn east (right) and follow it for 5.3 miles to the end of the tour. This route is 23 miles long.

Lunch stop

7 West Lakes

MAP 5
PAGE 37

Difficulty	2
Length	Up to 4 miles round trip
Elevation	7250/Up to +350, −350
Navigation	Map
Time	Few hours
Season	December through April
USGS topo	15′ series, Donner Pass
Start	At the plowed loading zone on the north side of Highway 80 at the Castle Peak Area and Boreal Ridge exit. Parking is available at the east end of the frontage road which is on the south side of the highway.

You will find excellent touring terrain to the north of Highway 80 in the vicinity of West Lakes. This area is filled with small and rolling hills. When it is raining in Truckee, consider driving up here where it is probably snowing. The nearby slopes can provide hours of pleasurable telemark practice.

Begin this tour by skiing for 0.1 mile east on a road parallel to the highway. Continue on the road for 0.1 mile as it begins to turn northwest. You will probably see a well-used trail along the road which is described in the Round Valley and Peter Grubb Hut tour.

Instead of following the beaten path, leave the road and ski northeast where you can explore at your leisure. Summit Lake is an excellent objective. The tour to Summit Lake and then to Euer Valley is described in the Boreal Ridge to Euer Valley tour.

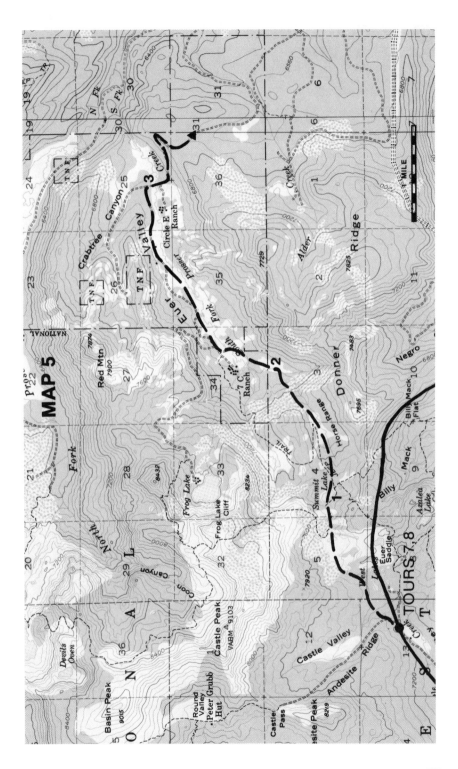

MAP 5

37

8 Boreal Ridge to Euer Valley

MAP 5
PAGE 37

Difficulty	3
Length	7 miles one-way
Elevation	7200/+450, −950
Navigation	Road, map and compass
Time	Full day
Season	Late December through mid-April
USGS topo	15′ series, Donner Pass
Start	At the plowed loading zone on the north side of Highway 80 at the Castle Peak Area and Boreal Ridge exit. Parking is available at the east end of the frontage road which is on the south side of the highway.
End	Alder Creek Road where it is no longer plowed. From Donner Pass Road in Truckee drive north along Northwood Blvd. for 4.0 miles. Turn right onto Fjord Road and after 0.1 mile turn left onto Alder Creek Road. Drive 0.8 mile to the end of the plowed road. Be aware that in recent years it has not been legal to park here.

This tour is chuck-full of all the good things which ski touring has to offer. You can find perfect rolling terrain, some downhill, and long flats, and you can test your ability with a compass as you ski through woods and open areas.

Begin this tour by skiing for 0.1 mile east on a road parallel to the highway. Continue on the road for 0.1 mile as it begins to turn northwest. You will probably see a well-used trail along the road which is described in the Round Valley and Peter Grubb Hut tour.

Instead of following the beaten path, leave the road and ski northeast. Since there are no markers or roads to follow, you will need to refer often to your map and compass. Your first goal is to reach Summit Lake (1) which is 1.7 miles away. The route is over open, rolling terrain which is interspersed with some creek and gully crossings and some woods. Summit Lake itself is surrounded by trees and can be difficult to locate. If necessary, climb above the trees to spot it.

Once you reach Summit Lake, the route-finding becomes significantly easier. Ski east by following the drainage which descends to the South Fork of Prosser Creek. Drop gradually for 0.7 mile to a meadow. From the meadow, ski east for 0.3 mile to a point where you must descend 400′ in 0.4 mile to a lake (2) which is shown as a meadow on the topo. In this last section, stay to the north of the creek.

Ski to the north end of the lake and then through the trees for 0.1 mile to the edge of the meadow in Euer Valley. At this point, you are on the south side of Prosser Creek which you can follow northeast through Euer Valley. You can also cross to the north side of the creek on either a very small footbridge or a snowbridge. Regardless of which side you ski on, follow the South Fork of Prosser Creek to the northeast for 2.0 miles until you find a large bridge **(3)**.

From the bridge, ski southeast on the road which ascends 200′ out of the valley. At the high point, follow the unplowed road or telephone line to the end of the tour.

New snow on a cold, crisp morning

9 Donner Memorial State Park

MAP 6
PAGE 41

Difficulty	1
Length	2 miles round trip
Elevation	5950/Nil
Navigation	Marked trail
Time	Few hours
Season	Late December through March
USGS topo	15′ series, Truckee, Donner Pass
Start	Park at the museum at Donner Memorial State Park which is located at the east end of Donner Lake. Walk to the entrance building of the campground (closed in winter) and the trailhead is located just beyond.

Donner Memorial State Park is a perfect place to enjoy a few hours of a winter afternoon. The tour is level, well-marked, and popular among beginners. While you are there, you can also visit the park museum and learn about the saga of California pioneers.

Begin the tour by skiing downhill on a road for 25 yards to Donner Creek. Cross the creek on a bridge and continue for another 25 yards to a fork in the road. Take the west (right) fork and ski for 1.1 miles along the south shore of Donner Lake to China Cove (1). Here a marker indicates the point where the ski touring trail leaves the road.

Follow the marked trail to the east (left) for 0.5 mile until you intersect a snow-covered road. Ski east on the road for 0.4 mile until the road turns north. Continue on the road for 0.3 mile to Donner Creek and the end of the tour.

You can lengthen this tour by skiing along the south shore of Donner Lake west of China Cove. Do not ski on the lake itself since it is never stable.

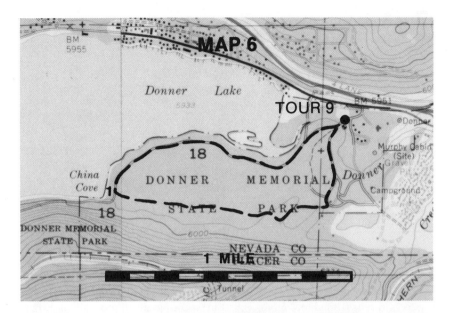

Railroad tracks in Coldstream Valley

10 Coldstream Valley

MAP 7
PAGE 43

Difficulty	2–4
Length	Up to 12 miles round trip
Elevation	5950/Up to +1250/−1250
Navigation	Road and map
Time	Up to full day
Season	Late December through March
USGS topo	15' series, Truckee, Donner Pass
Start	Just south of Highway 80 where Donner Pass Road crosses it. This is about three miles west of the center of Truckee. Park near the entrance to the gravel pit.

This tour takes you through the historically rich Coldstream Valley, over a beautiful section of the Emigrant Trail on which pioneers crossed the Sierra Nevada in search of gold and a new life, and alongside railroad tracks laid over 100 years ago as part of the transcontinental railroad. This era is captured at the nearby Donner Memorial State Park museum.

Skiers of all abilities can enjoy a tour through Coldstream Valley. The first 3.5 miles climb only 350' to Horseshoe Bend. Advancing beginners can ski as far as they desire and then retrace their route. More advanced skiers can continue up Cold Creek to the bowl below Mt. Lincoln. The corniced ridge above the bowl is visible as you ski through Coldstream Valley.

You must consider two factors when planning to tour here: First, the tour is at a very low elevation and may be a poor choice in periods of low snowfall. Second, you must evaluate the avalanche conditions and be very cautious if you are planning to ski in the bowl below Mt. Lincoln.

You begin this tour just past the entrance to the gravel pit on a snow-covered road which heads south. Ski on this road for 0.3 mile until you reach a junction (1) where you take the east (left) fork. Ski for another 0.2 mile until the road begins to climb. Climb at a steep angle for another 0.2 mile until the road levels (2). Follow the level road as it continues up the valley until the road appears to end at the railroad tracks. Either ski alongside or slightly below the tracks for 0.2 mile until you reach Horseshoe Bend (3).

From Horseshoe Bend, continue up Cold Creek. You should follow the creek to the southwest and then to the west since the road may not be visible. As mentioned earlier, this part of the tour is for more advanced skiers and is not safe when unstable snow conditions exist.

A variation of this tour is to ski from Horseshoe Bend to Eder and descend Lakeview Canyon to Donner Lake. The Schallenberger Loop tour describes that route.

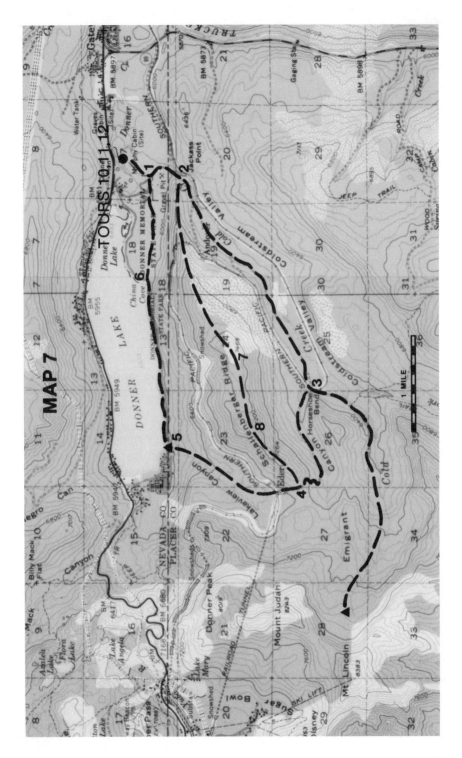

MAP 7

TOURS 10,11,12

43

MAP 7
PAGE 43

11 Schallenberger Loop

Difficulty	4
Length	7 miles one-way or 10 miles round trip
Elevation	5950/ + 900, − 900
Navigation	Road and map
Time	Full day
Season	January through March
USGS topo	15′ series, Truckee, Donner Pass
Start	Just south of Highway 80 where Donner Pass Road crosses it. This is about three miles west of the center of Truckee. Park near the entrance to the gravel pit.
End	Southwest end of Donner Lake on or near South Shore Drive about 0.7 mile south of Donner Pass Road. Make sure you park legally. If you park on other than South Shore Drive a street map may be useful in locating your car at the conclusion of the tour. It is also possible to end the tour at the starting point as described in the tour description.

This tour loops around Schallenberger Ridge by combining an easy tour up Coldstream Valley with more challenging skiing in Emigrant and Lakeview Canyons. The most difficult section is the final descent through the dense trees of Lakeview Canyon to Donner Lake.

Start this tour by following the Coldstream Valley tour (no. 10) for 3.5 miles to Horseshoe Bend (**3**). You should ski or walk alongside the railroad tracks as you approach the bend. Just before you reach the bend, the tracks cross the creek which drains Emigrant Canyon. Continue southwest along the tracks for 100 yards where, if you look carefully, you can find a road on the west (right) side of the tracks.

Ski south on this road for 50 yards and then turn north (right) onto a road which gradually turns west up Emigrant Canyon. Follow the road across the creek in Emigrant Canyon and up the canyon for 1.0 mile until the slopes to the north become less steep. Turn north and climb to a saddle (**4**). Be aware that you may find it difficult to follow the road in Emigrant Canyon.

From the saddle, ski 0.2 mile north until you intersect the railroad tracks; be cautious of the steep drop as you approach the tracks. Eder, a fuel and water stop for locomotives, once existed here. Nearby you will see several of the snowsheds which protect portions of the Southern Pacific Railroad tracks.

Cross to the north side of the tracks where you must descend a short but very steep slope. Once down the slope, ski gradually down Lakeview

Canyon through the trees for 0.9 mile. Finally you must descend at a steep angle through very dense woods for 0.4 mile to the houses located at Donner Lake **(5)**. You have completed this tour if your shuttle car is located here; otherwise you have two choices for returning to the starting point.

To return to the starting point you must first reach China Cove **(6)**. To reach the cove, ski east along the shore of Donner Lake for 1.7 miles. An alternative is to walk east on South Shore Drive for 1.3 miles until the road is no longer plowed. Then ski east on the road until it turns north at China Cove.

Regardless of the route you choose, at China Cove locate the marked ski trail through Donner Memorial State Park. Follow the trail (not the road along the lake) east for 0.5 mile until you intersect a snow-covered road. Ski east on the road for 0.4 mile until the road turns north. Where it turns north, continue east for 0.2 mile until you intersect the first road **(1)** on which you skied. Turn north (left) and follow the road for 0.3 mile back to the starting point.

A great day with friends   *Lee Griffith*

12 Schallenberger Ridge

MAP 7
PAGE 43

Difficulty	4
Length	10 miles round trip
Elevation	5950/ + 1700, − 1700
Navigation	Road and map
Time	Full day
Season	Late December through March
USGS topo	15′ series, Truckee, Donner Pass
Start	Just south of Highway 80 where Donner Pass Road crosses it. This is about three miles west of the center of Truckee. Park near the entrance to the gravel pit.

From north of Donner Lake on Highway 80, you can see the entire length of Schallenberger Ridge. Pick a clear day to ski along the ridge when you can appreciate the locale and the outstanding scenery. To the north and directly below the ridge is Donner Lake. Farther north lie ridges which hide Euer and Carpenter Valleys. To the southwest is the Mt. Lincoln-Anderson Peak ridge with its cornices and bowls. To the southeast is Coldstream Valley through which you ski to the end of this tour.

Begin this tour just past the entrance to the gravel pit and ski south on a snow-covered road for 0.3 mile until you reach a junction (1) where you take the east (left) fork. Continue on the road for 0.2 mile and then climb for another 0.2 mile until the road levels (2). Here, leave the road which continues up Coldstream Valley.

From the road, climb west up the steep east shoulder of Schallenberger Ridge which is easy to follow if you keep heading up. The terrain along the ridge is a combination of wooded and open areas. When choosing your route, remember to stay back from the north edge of the ridge where it may be overhung.

Once you leave the road behind, begin a steady climb. The bad news is that you must climb 1400′ in just 2.0 miles to the summit of Peak 7469 (7); the good news is that when you reach the top, you have done almost all of the elevation gain for the loop. On the way up, you cross a snow-covered road, and at one point, you can see where the railroad tracks below the ridge disappear into the mountainside.

From Peak 7469, descend and then ascend gradually to the west for 0.7 mile to the next peak (8). Continue by descending for 0.5 mile to the southwest along a much narrower portion of the ridge to Peak 7264 (a high but not prominent point). Although there is adequate space on this ridge to ski, remember that the north edges may be overhung.

Finally you descend 400′ in 0.4 mile through trees to a saddle (4) where you may be able to locate the road shown on the topo. To the north of the saddle is Eder, former site of a railroad stop. From the saddle, this tour heads south although you can reach Donner Lake by skiing north following the Schallenberger Loop tour.

From the saddle, ski south into Emigrant Canyon by following the road if possible. Once you are in the canyon, follow the road or creek to the east. At the east end of Emigrant Canyon, cross to the south side of the creek. From here, follow the road south to the railroad tracks at Horseshoe Bend **(3)**.

Now ski or walk along the railroad tracks to a point just northeast of the creek draining Emigrant Canyon. Drop down to the southeast of the tracks, and then ski northeast and parallel to them. As you ski, look carefully for a road which parallels the tracks. You now follow this road on which you began the tour for 3.3 miles through Coldstream Valley to the starting point.

Enjoying the views   *Lee Griffith*

13 Alder Creek Road

MAP 8
PAGE 48

Difficulty	1
Length	Short
Elevation	6700/Nil
Navigation	Adjacent to plowed road
Time	Short
Season	Mid-December through early April
USGS topo	15' series, Donner Pass
Start	Alder Creek Road where it is no longer plowed. From Donner Pass Road in Truckee drive north along Northwood Blvd. for 4.0 miles. Turn right onto Fjord Road and after 0.1 mile turn left onto Alder Creek Road. Drive 0.8 mile to the end of the plowed road. Be aware that in recent years it has not been legal to park here.

In a 0.5 mile radius of the starting point, the terrain, filled with flat sections and mild hills, is excellent for beginners to practice on. From the starting point, be sure to ski 0.3 mile over the unplowed road by following the telephone line to the rim overlooking Euer Valley. The view of three-mile-long Euer Valley is impressive.

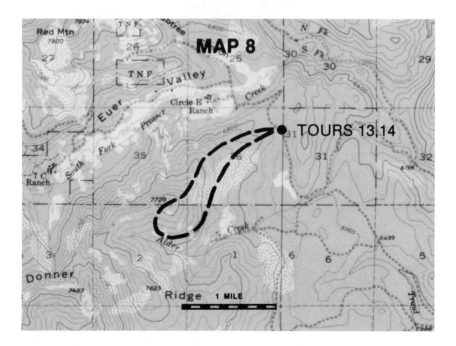

MAP 8
PAGE 48

Euer Ridge 14

Difficulty	3
Length	3 miles round trip
Elevation	6700/+1000, −1000
Navigation	Map
Time	Few hours
Season	Mid-December through early April
USGS topo	15' series, Donner Pass
Start	Alder Creek Road where it is no longer plowed. From Donner Pass Road in Truckee drive north along Northwood Blvd. for 4.0 miles. Turn right onto Fjord Road and after 0.1 mile turn left onto Alder Creek Road. Drive 0.8 mile to the end of the plowed road. Be aware that in recent years it has not been legal to park here.

This tour is a short, moderately steep climb to the summit of Peak 7729 which is the highest point of a short, unnamed ridge called Euer Ridge in this guidebook due to the prominence of Euer Valley lying to its north. If you have never skied to the summit of a peak and desire to do so, this tour is a good choice because the distance is short, the terrain is moderate, and the navigation is straightforward. Advanced skiers can enjoy a wide range of downhill terrain.

From the starting point, you can clearly see Peak 7729 to the southwest. Ski 1.4 miles to the summit of the peak along its northeast ridge. In the steepest sections, the trees offer some protection from avalanche danger. An alternative route to the summit is to follow the direct route of the power lines which ascend to a point just south of the summit.

Both during the climb and at the summit, you can see many prominent landmarks. To the north is Euer Valley and to its north is Red Mountain. Two routes to the summit of Red Mountain are described in this guidebook. To the southeast are the barren slopes of Tahoe Donner Ski Resort, and to the southwest is Donner Ridge.

To return to the starting point, you can retrace your route or take an alternate route which is considerably less steep. To follow the alternate route, descend to the southwest through sparse trees toward Alder Creek. At an appropriate elevation, about 100' above the creek, start to traverse east and continue around Peak 7729. Lose elevation gradually as you traverse. Once you are on the east side of the peak, you can see the power lines to the north. Ski to the power lines and then follow them back to the starting point.

Ridge between Peak 7874 and Red Mountain

MAP 9
PAGE 53

Euer Valley **15**

Difficulty	2
Length	3 to 8 miles round trip
Elevation	6700/+200, −200
Navigation	Road
Time	Half day
Season	Mid-December through early April
USGS topo	15′ series, Donner Pass
Start	Alder Creek Road where it is no longer plowed. From Donner Pass Road in Truckee drive north along Northwood Blvd. for 4.0 miles. Turn right onto Fjord Road and after 0.1 mile turn left onto Alder Creek Road. Drive 0.8 mile to the end of the plowed road. Be aware that in recent years it has not been legal to park here.

The route to Euer Valley, unlike other tours to a valley, takes you first to the rim overlooking the valley and then to the valley floor. From the rim, you are treated to an impressive view of three-mile-long Euer Valley and the South Fork of Prosser Creek running its length.

From the starting point, ski north for 0.3 mile over the unplowed road by following the telephone line to the rim above Euer Valley. Continue on the road as it descends 200′ in 1.0 mile to the South Fork of Prosser Creek which you cross on a bridge (**1**).

From the north side of the creek, you can follow the road, which may be difficult to do, for 2.3 miles up the valley. If you cannot distinguish the road, you can ski along the creek instead. From the north side of the bridge, you can also ski 0.5 mile down the valley.

Be aware that Euer Valley is private property, and the owner has the right to exclude tourers although this policy has not been enforced in the past.

16 Frog Lake

MAP 9 PAGE 53

MAP 9
PAGE 53

Difficulty	3
Length	12 miles round trip
Elevation	6700/+1500, −1500
Navigation	Road, map and compass
Time	Full day
Season	Mid-December through early April
USGS topo	15' series, Donner Pass
Start	Alder Creek Road where it is no longer plowed. From Donner Pass Road in Truckee drive north along Northwood Blvd. for 4.0 miles. Turn right onto Fjord Road and after 0.1 mile turn left onto Alder Creek Road. Drive 0.8 mile to the end of the plowed road. Be aware that in recent years it has not been legal to park here.

Frog Lake is situated at the very base of the impressive 500' vertical face of Frog Lake Cliff and is reached by an extension of the Euer Valley tour.

Start this tour by following the directions in the Euer Valley tour (no. 15) to the bridge (1) across the South Fork of Prosser Creek. Cross to the north side of the creek and then ski up the valley on the road or along the creek for 2.0 miles. Next you should look very carefully for the road (2) which heads north to Frog Lake.

Climb on this narrow road for 1.4 miles to a broad clearing (3) where the road disappears. Continue up the clearing for about 0.2 mile and then ski west through dense trees for 0.8 mile to Frog Lake.

Be aware that both Euer Valley and Frog Lake are private property, and the owner has the right to exclude tourers although this policy has not been enforced in the past.

Red Mountain

MAP 9
PAGE 53

17 Red Mountain Traverse

Difficulty	5
Length	9 miles round trip
Elevation	6700/ + 2100, − 2100
Navigation	Map and compass
Time	Full day
Season	Mid-December through early April
USGS topo	15′ series, Donner Pass
Start	Alder Creek Road where it is no longer plowed. From Donner Pass Road in Truckee drive north along Northwood Blvd. for 4.0 miles. Turn right onto Fjord Road and after 0.1 mile turn left onto Alder Creek Road. Drive 0.8 mile to the end of the plowed road. Be aware that in recent years it has not been legal to park here.

Red Mountain is situated on the ridge which separates Euer and Carpenter Valleys. From Euer Valley, the ascent of Red Mountain is a steep 1.5 mile climb; in one section you climb 1200′ in 1.2 miles. However, the real difficulty of this tour may not be this ascent but rather finding the base of the ridge in Crabtree Canyon which you must ascend.

The trudge up Red Mountain is made enjoyable by superb views. With a map and compass you can locate many landmarks in the area. This tour also features a traverse of impressive Red Mountain, first ascending from the east and then descending to the west.

If you are interested in this tour, you may also be interested in the Red Mountain from Carpenter Valley tour, a loop which also takes you to the summit.

In this tour, your first objective is to reach the bridge (1) which crosses the South Fork of Prosser Creek. Refer to the Euer Valley tour (no. 15) for directions to the bridge.

From the bridge, your next objective is to reach the base of the ridge (4) in Crabtree Canyon. The topo map shows a road heading north and then northwest from the bridge to the ridge. Although the road is probably not visible, carefully navigate to follow this route for 0.8 mile until the road turns west up an unnamed canyon while Crabtree Canyon continues northwest. Between the two canyons is the ridge you want to ascend. Although the ridge may be difficult to find due to trees in the canyon which hide it, locate its base.

Climb the ridge to the northwest, where the terrain is interspersed with clearings and wooded areas, for 0.8 mile until you reach a short level section.

From the level section, you must climb at a very steep angle to the summit of Peak 7874 **(5)** which is best approached from its northeast. From the peak, you can see Red Mountain to the southwest and much of the ridge between them. The cliffs on the north side of this section of ridge are very steep and normally very heavily corniced.

From the summit of Peak 7874, descend a short distance to the south and then traverse west to the saddle between the peak and Red Mountain. From the saddle, ascend Red Mountain **(6)** along the ridge line. Since this section is very steep and often icy, be extra careful; also stay away from the north edge which may be corniced. If necessary, take off your skis and hike this short distance. Once on the summit, take some time to locate the landmarks which surround you.

To descend from Red Mountain, ski west to the saddle **(7)** which separates Euer and Carpenter Valleys. From the saddle, ski south through more gentle terrain for 0.9 mile to a point where the terrain becomes steep and densely wooded **(3)**. Here it is important to locate the road to Euer Valley, the location of which is not obvious. Carefully look for it on the east (left) side of the drainage. Follow this road for 1.3 miles to Euer Valley **(2)**.

Once in Euer Valley, ski northeast through it for 2.0 miles to the bridge **(1)** across the South Fork of Prosser Creek. You complete the tour by climbing out of the valley on the road on which the tour began.

View from Red Mountain

18 Carpenter Valley

MAP 10
PAGE 59

Difficulty	1–2
Length	5 to 11 miles round trip
Elevation	6200/ + 100, – 100
Navigation	Road
Time	Half to full day
Season	Late December through March
USGS topo	15' series, Truckee, Donner Pass
Start	Intersection of Alder Creek Road and Carpenter Valley Road. From the Sierraville-Quincy exit on Highway 80 or from Truckee, drive 2.4 miles north of Highway 80 on Highway 89. Turn left on Alder Creek Road and after 2.9 miles unplowed Carpenter Valley Road will be on the right. Do not expect to find a street sign for Carpenter Valley Road.

The Carpenter Valley area is becoming increasingly popular as people discover it. The gentle terrain and easy-to-follow road make this area particularly suitable for inexperienced skiers. You can custom tailor this tour by traveling a distance of your choice up the three-mile-long valley. The distance from the starting point to the valley is 2.6 miles.

From the starting point, ski northwest on the level, snow-covered road for 0.5 mile. Next you gradually descend for 0.6 mile to Prosser Creek. Continue on the road for 0.5 until you cross the South Fork of Prosser Creek on a bridge. In this area, the barren, fire-scarred hillsides are not a pretty sight, but the scenery quickly improves.

Continue on the road for 0.4 mile until you reach a road junction (1) where the woods begin. At the junction, take the north (right) fork and follow the level road through the trees for 0.6 mile to the edge of Carpenter Valley.

Once you reach Carpenter Valley, you can ski as far as you desire. There is no need to follow the road; in fact, where the road is supposed to cross the North Fork of Prosser Creek, according to the topo, there is not even a bridge. If you want to cross the creek, you must find a snowbridge. You should also notice that there is a small section of woods which divides the valley into two meadows.

Be aware that most of Carpenter Valley belongs to the American Sportsman Club. Please respect their property rights.

MAP **10**
PAGE 59

Crabtree Canyon Ridge **19**

Difficulty	3
Length	6 to 9 miles round trip
Elevation	6200/Up to + 1050, − 1050
Navigation	Road and map
Time	Up to full day
Season	Late December through March
USGS topo	15′ series, Truckee, Donner Pass
Start	Intersection of Alder Creek Road and Carpenter Valley Road. From the Sierraville-Quincy exit on Highway 80 or from Truckee, drive 2.4 miles north of Highway 80 on Highway 89. Turn left on Alder Creek Road and after 2.9 miles unplowed Carpenter Valley Road will be on the right. Do not expect to find a street sign for Carpenter Valley Road.

This tour takes you to the broad ridge between Carpenter Valley and Crabtree Canyon where you make your own route up the ridge through open areas as well as through wooded spots. The unnamed ridge, called Crabtree Canyon Ridge in this guidebook, is a pleasant place to spend the afternoon enjoying splendid views.

Begin this tour by following the Carpenter Valley tour (no. 18) to a road junction (1) where Carpenter Valley Road enters the woods. At the junction, the north (right) fork leads to Carpenter Valley; instead take the south (left) fork and climb at a steep angle for 0.9 mile to a point (2) at the northeast end of Euer Valley. This point is just to the north of the South Fork of Prosser Creek where the creek descends from Euer Valley to the North Fork of Prosser Creek.

The road you have been following now continues west (not shown on the topo) into Euer Valley; for this tour, you turn northwest and follow the ridge located between Carpenter Valley and Crabtree Canyon. Climb steadily along the ridge for as far as you desire while enjoying the views along the way.

This tour returns to the starting point by retracing the route described above. An alternate but much more difficult route is to make a loop which includes an ascent of Red Mountain. That route is described in the Red Mountain from Carpenter Valley tour.

20 Red Mountain from Carpenter Valley

MAP 10
PAGE 59

Difficulty	5
Length	12 miles round trip
Elevation	6200/ + 2100, − 2100
Navigation	Road, map and compass
Time	Full day
Season	Late December through March
USGS topo	15′ series, Truckee, Donner Pass
Start	Intersection of Alder Creek Road and Carpenter Valley Road. From the Sierraville-Quincy exit on Highway 80 or from Truckee, drive 2.4 miles north of Highway 80 on Highway 89. Turn left on Alder Creek Road and after 2.9 miles unplowed Carpenter Valley Road will be on the right. Do not expect to find a street sign for Carpenter Valley Road.

A tour to the summit of Red Mountain is a formidable undertaking which rewards you with countless dramatic views. While both this tour and the Red Mountain Traverse tour lead you to the summit, this longer one is slightly less steep.

Your first objective is to reach the ridge which you follow to Red Mountain and which is described in the Crabtree Canyon Ridge tour (no. 19). Follow the directions for that tour to the point (2) at the northeast end of Euer Valley.

Continue by ascending the ridge which heads northwest, then west, and finally southwest for 2.6 miles until you reach the summit of Peak 7874 (3). From the summit, you can see Red Mountain to the southwest and the ridge connecting Peak 7874 with Red Mountain. The north side of that section of ridge is very steep and is usually heavily corniced.

From Peak 7874, descend a short distance to the south and then traverse west to the saddle between the peak and Red Mountain. Ascend along the ridge line to the summit of Red Mountain; be sure to stay back from the north edge which may be overhung. You may want to hike this last section if the route is icy; you do not have to carry your skis to the summit because the return route descends from the saddle.

Return to the saddle between Peak 7874 and Red Mountain. From the saddle, descend southeast along the steep gully for 0.4 mile until the terrain becomes more level and the gully turns east into a drainage. Continue for 0.6 mile down the drainage until you pick up a road. Continue to follow the road down the drainage for 0.5 mile to Crabtree Canyon.

Once you are in Crabtree Canyon follow the road southeast for 0.5 mile. If you continue to follow the road, you eventually arrive at the bridge which crosses the South Fork of Prosser Creek in Euer Valley. Instead, where the terrain becomes fairly level **(4)**, turn east (left) off the road. Continue east for 0.7 mile until you reach the base of the ridge **(2)** at the northeast end of Euer Valley which you ascended at the beginning of the tour, or until you reach a road which leads you to this base. From the base, ski 2.9 miles back to the starting point.

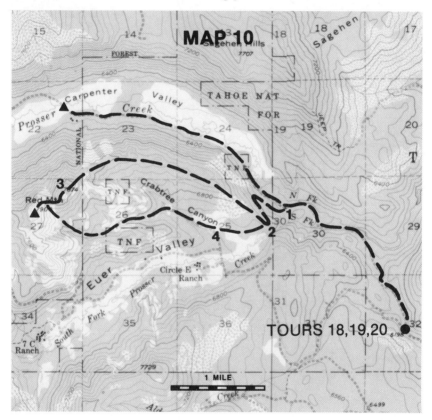

Final ascent of Red Mountain

North Tahoe

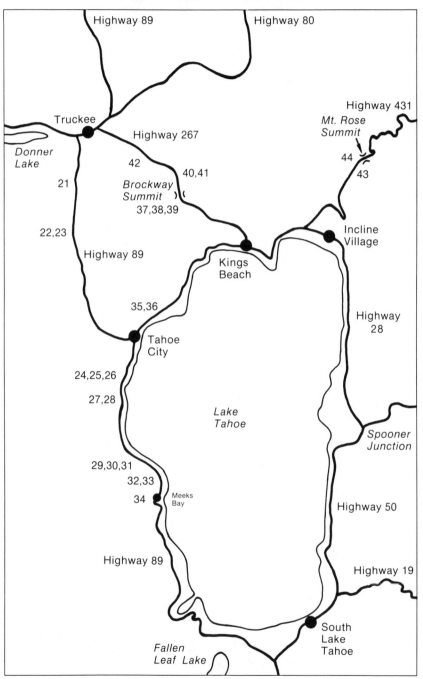

Highway 89

Highway 80

Highway 431

Mt. Rose
Summit

44

43

Truckee

Highway 267

Donner
Lake

42

21

40,41

Brockway
Summit

37,38,39

Incline
Village

22,23

Highway 89

Kings
Beach

35,36

Highway
28

Tahoe
City

24,25,26

27,28

Lake
Tahoe

Spooner
Junction

29,30,31

32,33

34

Meeks
Bay

Highway 50

Highway 89

Highway 19

Fallen
Leaf Lake

South
Lake
Tahoe

21 Cabin Creek Loop

MAP 11
PAGE 63

Difficulty	3
Length	4 miles round trip
Elevation	6250/ + 700, − 700
Navigation	Marked trail, road and map
Time	Half day
Season	Late December through March
USGS topo	15′ series, Truckee
Start	Near the Sanitary Land Fill which is located on Cabin Creek Road. From Highway 80 drive south for 3.2 miles on Highway 89. Turn northwest onto Cabin Creek Road and drive 1.0 mile until the road levels where you will find a snow-covered road on the west side of Cabin Creek Road. This point is marked with a Forest Service ski touring sign. If you reach the dump you have gone too far.

The Cabin Creek Loop is a short tour with a little bit of everything, including fine views from the breaks in the woods. Most of the tour is on snow-covered roads although there is one cross-country section along a creek drainage.

The 1955 Truckee 15′ series topo does not show any of the roads which are used in this tour, and unfortunately the 1955 Truckee 7.5′ series topo is no better. While most of the route is marked, the markers most needed are hard to find, so it is necessary to carefully follow the tour description.

From the starting point, ski west on the snow-covered road for 0.2 mile to a junction (1) where the loop begins and ends. You return to this point on the road from the south (left). Begin the loop by skiing north (right) on the road for 0.4 mile until you pass the disposal site on your right. At this point, you may see a marker on the west (left) side of the road indicating that the marked trail leaves the road. Instead stay on the road and continue north on it for another 0.4 mile to a road junction (2).

At the junction, make a sharp turn to the west (left) and continue on the road for 0.4 mile to still another road junction (3). At this junction, continue on the south (left) fork for 0.3 mile until the road makes a sharp turn northwest. At this point, the marked trail is supposed to intersect this route once again.

Continue on the road for 0.4 mile where you make a sharp turn to the south (left) with the road. You can get good views toward Truckee by skiing off the road to the northeast just before you make the turn. Continue on the road to the south, then southwest, and pass to the north of Peak 7113 (4). Up to this point, you have been climbing steadily, but here the road crests and begins to descend. From this point, you can see Anderson Peak straight ahead.

From the crest, continue southwest on the road for 0.2 mile until you can see a drainage leading southeast. Leave the road and gradually turn southeast while descending into the drainage. You can also continue down the road for 0.3 mile to its lowest point, then leave the road, and descend southeast.

Regardless of the route you take, ski southeast down the drainage and parallel to the creek on its north side until the terrain steepens and you encounter an old, rock-covered roadbed which is marginal for skiing early and late in the season. The manzanita bordering the road can also make skiing poor, and you may find the best skiing on the south side of the creek. Whichever side you choose, continue down the creek until you reach a road at a bridge **(5)**.

From the bridge, ski north (left) on the road for 0.3 mile until you reach the first road junction **(1)**. Turn east (right) and ski 0.2 mile back to the starting point.

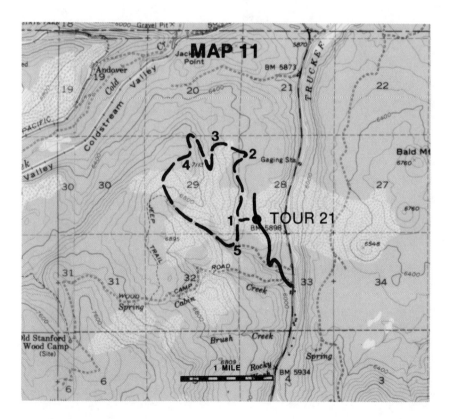

Steep descent

MAP 12
PAGE 67

Pole Creek Loop 22

Difficulty	3
Length	4 miles round trip
Elevation	6000/+650, −650
Navigation	Road
Time	Few hours
Season	Late December through mid-April
USGS topo	15′ series, Tahoe; 7.5′ series, Tahoe City
Start	Big Chief Lodge on Highway 89, 6.5 miles south of Highway 80 and 8.0 miles north of Tahoe City.

This short, easy-to-follow tour has considerable elevation gain. A little fresh snow helps give you confidence to enjoy the quick descent. Easy access, a road to follow, and protection from the wind make this tour ideal for bad weather conditions.

You may find that parking is very limited at the starting point. If you cannot find legal parking along the highway, you can park at Big Chief Guides ski touring center which is adjacent to the lodge. It solicits donations for parking, trail maps, and trail maintenance.

Pole Creek crosses Highway 89 just south of Big Chief Lodge. On the south side of the creek and on the west side of the highway, find the snow-covered road which you ascend for 1.7 miles to a road junction (1). The west (left) fork heads to Silver Creek; instead take the north (right) fork and descend gradually for 0.5 mile to a bridge across Pole Creek (2).

Cross the bridge to the north side of the creek and encounter a road junction. If you want to lengthen the tour, turn west (left) and follow the road as far as you desire. The road climbs steadily and at a steep angle for 2.6 miles to a very distinct meadow. Along the route there are two road junctions. From the junction at the bridge, travel 0.9 mile to the first road junction and stay left. Continue for another 1.6 miles to a second road junction and stay right. The meadow is 0.1 mile ahead. Beware of avalanche conditions in the vicinity of the meadow.

From the bridge (2), the Pole Creek Loop tour continues on the road to the east (right). Ski on the road which parallels the creek on its north side for 1.1 miles back to Highway 89. This return route is a continuous downhill run, and the final 0.2 mile drops at a very steep angle. If the snow is in poor condition, you may find it a good idea to walk this stretch. When you reach the highway, you are 0.2 mile north of Big Chief Lodge.

You can also ski the loop in the reverse direction, making the uphill steeper but the downhill more gradual. Another alternative is to follow the route described to Pole Creek and return via that same route. Although the distance is a little longer, the skiing is easier.

Difficulty	4
Length	10 miles round trip
Elevation	6000/+2400, −2400
Navigation	Road and map
Time	Full day
Season	Late December through March
USGS topo	15′ series, Tahoe; 7.5′ series, Tahoe City
Start	Big Chief Lodge on Highway 89, 6.5 miles south of Highway 80 and 8.0 miles north of Tahoe City.

From the small summit of Silver Peak, the views are magnificent in all directions. You can see Squaw Valley Ski Resort to the south, only 1.6 miles away but more than 2000′ below. There are also excellent views of Lake Tahoe from both the ascent route and the summit.The tour to the summit is for advanced skiers who seek either the summit of a windswept peak or excellent telemark terrain. If telemarking is your goal, pick a time when the snow is fresh or when spring conditions exist. Due to the elevation and orientation of the final ascent route, the snow near the summit tends to stay good for a considerable time after a new snowfall. Much of this tour, however, is through avalanche terrain, and you must exercise appropriate care.

Start the tour by following the Pole Creek Loop tour (no. 22) for 1.7 miles to a road junction (1) where roads branch out in different directions to Pole Creek and Silver Creek. Take the west (left) fork, climb gradually for 0.9 mile, and then climb at a steeper angle for 0.5 mile to an obvious overlook point (3). From the overlook, the excellent views include a view of Silver Peak to the west.

Continue skiing on the road to the northwest for 0.3 mile until you reach an obscure fork in the road (4). The obvious road, which continues straight ahead, is part of the Saddle Trail and is marked by Big Chief Guides; instead follow the obscure road which makes a turn to the south (left) for 0.4 mile.

As you ski south on the road, you begin to traverse very steep terrain. Just before the road enters a bowl (5), which has a rock outcrop high above it on the ridge, leave the road and ski northwest up a broad ridge. When the broad ridge disappears, continue to climb to the northwest and to the summit of Silver Peak.

From the road, it is a 1000′ climb in 0.6 mile to the summit of Silver Peak. For safety, stay in the sparse trees where possible. If the snow near the top is wind-packed, leave your skis near the last trees and hike the final 150′ of elevation gain to the summit. Head for a rock outcrop just to the south of the peak from where you can see the summit. To the south of the actual summit is a wooden cross and the remains of a crashed airplane.

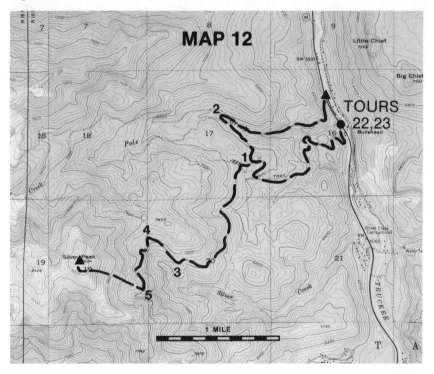

Winter trail

MAP 13
PAGE 71

Paige Meadows **24**

Difficulty	2
Length	1 to 4 miles round trip
Elevation	7000/ + 100, − 100
Navigation	Map
Time	Few hours
Season	December through mid-April
USGS topo	15′ series, Tahoe; 7.5′ series, Tahoe City
Start	This tour beings in Talmont Estates. From the Tahoe City Bridge drive south on Highway 89 for 1.9 miles. Turn right onto Pine Avenue, after 0.2 mile turn right onto Tahoe Park Heights, after 0.7 mile turn right onto Big Pine Drive, and after 0.3 mile turn left onto Silver Tip Drive. Drive 0.5 mile until Club Drive goes to the left and Silver Tip Drive is no longer plowed. Park here.

Paige Meadows is not one meadow but a series of half-a-dozen inter-connected meadows which have been protected from the sprawl of Lake Tahoe development. Beginners can appreciate the beauty of Sierra mead-ows in this scenic area. Because this area is slightly higher than the lo-cation of other beginner trails in the Lake Tahoe vicinity, you can enjoy more and better snow.

Where Silver Tip Drive appears to continue, ski for 0.1 mile to a distinct crest. Continue straight ahead and down an open area until you enter the woods. Continue in the same direction and quickly drop 75′. When your route becomes level, turn right and ski 50 yards through the trees to the edge of Paige Meadows.

Once you ski into a meadow, the next one becomes visible. Since this pattern continues with each adjacent meadow, you can explore any num-ber of them as you wish. For variation, ski in the woods which surround them.

Several notes are appropriate here: Most important, because of the multi-meadow configuration, take great care when entering Paige Mead-ows so that you can find your return route; it is easy to confuse the meadows, and there are often many ski tracks. If you have been to Paige Meadows before and are thoroughly confident of your route finding skills, Paige Meadows can be a pleasant location for a moonlight tour. Finally, when driving back to Highway 89, take a moment to admire Lake Tahoe from the intersection of Big Pine Drive and Tahoe Park Heights.

Difficulty	3
Length	9 miles round trip
Elevation	6800/+1700, −1700
Navigation	Road, map and compass
Time	Full day
Season	December through mid-April
USGS topo	15′ series Tahoe; 7.5′ series, Tahoe City
Start	From the bridge in Tahoe City, drive 2.5 miles south on Highway 89 to Pineland Drive. Turn right onto Pineland Drive and continue 0.4 mile until the road becomes Twin Peaks. Continue another 0.1 mile and the name of the road changes to Ward Creek Road. Drive 2.5 miles farther to Kitzbuhel Road (somewhere in this section Ward Creek Road will change name to Courcheval Road). Turn right onto Kitzbuhel and drive 0.2 mile to the dead end where the tour begins.

Although this tour is located in a wooded area near Tahoe City, it offers the peace and quiet of a more remote place. Although there are views of Paige Meadows and of Lake Tahoe along the route, the best ones are from the summit of Scott Peak where steep, corniced ridges to the north and west line the horizon. While it is not difficult to reach the summit, skiers who prefer a shorter tour can enjoy the rolling terrain near the starting point or a section of the tour.

Since this tour is predominantly on roads, only the very beginning and the final ascent require any navigation. The first 0.6 mile through woods without any landmarks poses the greatest difficulty.

From the starting point, ski east into the trees. Almost immediately you reach a clearing where you turn north. Shortly after you turn, cross a road and continue north where you pass through several small clearings. After skiing 0.4 mile from the starting point, you reach the largest clearing. From here you continue north for 0.2 mile until you intersect a road (**1**) which is more obvious in some places than in others.

The road you intersect heads east (right) to Paige Meadows. To continue to Scott Peak, follow the road to the west (left) for about 0.2 mile until it makes a sharp turn to the northeast (right). Continue on the road for 1.0 mile to a creek and for another 0.3 mile to a road junction (**2**).

At the junction, ski on the road which climbs to the northwest for 0.4 mile where you turn south with the road. Continue on the road for 0.4 mile to a junction (**3**) where you take the west (right) fork. Then continue another 0.4 mile to another junction (**4**) at a prominent saddle where you again take the west (right) fork.

Continue on the road for 0.4 mile until the road crosses an east-west ridge **(5)**. At this point, leave the road and climb steadily southwest to the saddle between Scott Peak and Peak 8208. Continue southwest for 0.2 mile to the summit of Scott Peak.

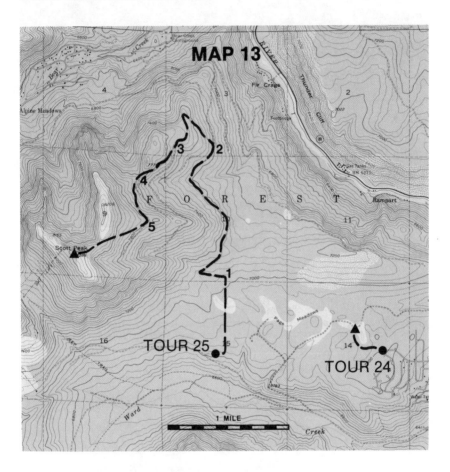

Creek crossing on a snowbridge

MAP **14**
PAGE 75

Stanford Rock **26**

Difficulty	3
Length	8 or 11 miles round trip
Elevation	6500/+2000, −2000 or 6300/+2200, −2200
Navigation	Road and map
Time	Full day
Season	Mid-December through April
USGS topo	15′ series, Tahoe; 7.5′ series, Tahoe City, Homewood
Start	From the bridge in Tahoe City, drive 2.5 miles south on Highway 89 to Pineland Drive. Turn right onto Pineland Drive and continue 0.4 mile until the road becomes Twin Peaks. Continue another 0.1 mile and the name of the road changes to Ward Creek Road. The starting point is exactly 0.9 mile ahead but do not expect to find parking here unless you bring a shovel. An alternate starting point is on Highway 89 on the south side of the bridge across Ward Creek, 0.4 mile south of Pineland Drive.

The tour to Stanford Rock offers spectacular views along the route as well as from the summit. When snow conditions are good, the continuous but moderate gradient offers a wonderful descent. However, if conditions are bad, this descent can be unpleasant due to icy spots on the narrow road. Plan to do this tour accordingly.

Ward Creek starting point. The only major challenge of this tour, crossing Ward Creek, is located at the beginning. In March 1985, there was a large tree across the creek on which you could cross. If you find walking across it uncomfortable or if it is gone, you can either puddle jump at low water levels, or you can start on Highway 89 at the Ward Creek bridge.

After crossing Ward Creek, ski south on the snow-covered road for 50 yards until you reach a road junction. The road to the east (left) is part of a road which zig-zags up to where the road to the south (straight) goes directly. Continue south for another 50 yards to another junction **(1)** where you cross the road which zig-zags and the route from Highway 89.

Highway 89 starting point. You can begin this tour at Highway 89 just south of the bridge across Ward Creek. From this starting point, ski west and parallel to Ward Creek. If you look carefully, you can find an abandoned road creating a clear path. About 0.4 mile from the start, the clear route disappears, and you should veer slightly south until you intersect a well-defined roadbed.

Continue west and parallel to the creek on this road until you intersect

26

a road which seems to make a switchback. Take the south (left) fork and follow it for 0.1 mile until a road (1), the route from Ward Creek, crosses the one you are on. Turn southwest (left) and pick up that route. Starting the tour on Highway 89 increases the length of the tour by 2.6 miles and $+200', -200'$.

From the intersection (1) of the routes from Ward Creek and Highway 89, continue southwest for 0.1 mile until the road turns east. Continue skiing east on the road for 0.5 mile to a fork (2) in the road. The north (left) fork leads to the Timberland subdivision but is not an acceptable ski route. The tour continues on the south (right) fork for 100 yards until you pass a very small road on your right.

Continue by following the road which turns south (right) for 0.3 mile until the road turns west (right). Climb gradually on it for 0.7 mile until you turn south (left) (3) with the road again.

Continue south on the road for 0.3 mile until you reach a relatively flat and open area where you must look carefully for the road leaving the high side of the clearing. From the clearing, continue on the road for 0.3 mile until you reach a ridge (4). In this last section between the clearing and the ridge, follow the road with care, especially when crossing an open area.

Cross the ridge and continue west on the road for 0.4 mile until it turns north. In this section, traverse above a steep slope, and just before the road turns north there is a spectacular view down into Blackwood Canyon.

Continue north on the road until you intersect a ridge (5). Follow the road along the ridge to the southwest for 0.1 mile. Then turn south and ski on the road for 0.4 mile until you reach a distinctive view point (6).

From the view point, you climb northwest for 300' in 0.3 mile to the summit of Stanford Rock. In this section, although you may not be able to discern the road, the route is obvious. At the summit, the striking view to the west is of Twin Peaks.

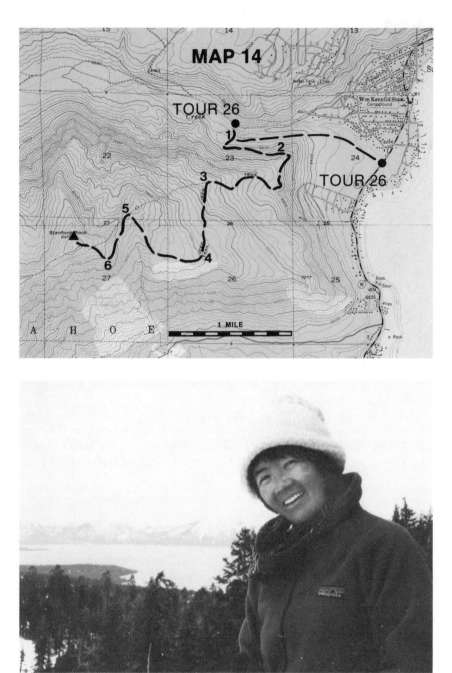

Lake Tahoe from Scott Peak

27 Blackwood Canyon

MAP 15
PAGE 77

Difficulty	1
Length	Up to 7 miles round trip
Elevation	6200/ + 200, − 200
Navigation	Road
Time	Half day
Season	Late December through early April
USGS topo	15′ series, Tahoe; 7.5′ series, Homewood
Start	Kaspian Recreation Area on Highway 89, 4.4 miles south of the bridge in Tahoe City.

Wooded Blackwood Canyon is over four miles long. Stanford Rock, Twin Peaks, Barker Peak, and Ellis Peak are prominent on the ridges which flank the canyon and form the large bowl at its head. When planning your trip, keep in mind that this area is often used by snowmobilers.

From the starting point, follow the snow-covered road west for 1.8 miles until you pass the north edge of a meadow. About a mile from the start, you can catch a glimpse of Twin Peaks if you look straight ahead where the road cuts through the trees. From the meadow's edge, continue west for another 0.4 mile until you reach a bridge which crosses Blackwood Creek **(1)**.

Beginners can either turn around at the bridge or continue to ski on the north side of the creek where the terrain remains level for another mile. If you cross the bridge, the road climbs steadily to Barker Pass. The tour to the pass is more difficult and is described in the Barker Pass tour.

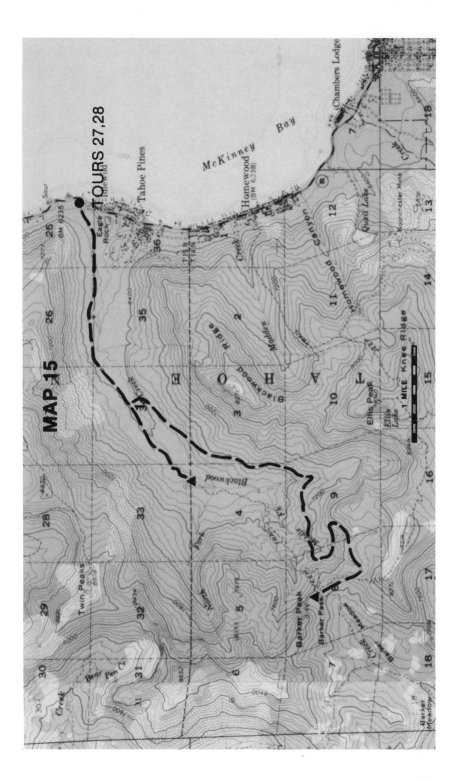

28 Barker Pass

MAP 15
PAGE 77

Difficulty	3
Length	14 miles round trip
Elevation	6200/ + 1500, − 1500
Navigation	Road
Time	Full day
Season	Late December through early April
USGS topo	15′ series, Tahoe; 7.5′ series, Homewood
Start	Kaspian Recreation Area on Highway 89, 4.4 miles south of the bridge in Tahoe City.

Barker Pass offers a fine view of Blackwood Canyon to the east and a glimpse of Lake Tahoe. The beautiful canyon is surrounded by Stanford Rock, Twin Peaks, Barker Peak, and Ellis Peak. To the west of the pass is Barker Meadow, and farther west is the Rubicon River.

The route to Barker Pass is on an easy-to-follow road. Follow the Blackwood Canyon tour (no. 27) for 2.2 miles to the bridge across Blackwood Creek **(1)**. Cross the bridge to the south side of the creek and climb at a steep angle on the road for 4.8 miles to Barker Pass.

Site of airplane crash on Silver Peak

MAP **16**
PAGE 81

Miller Meadows **29**

Difficulty	2
Length	8 miles round trip
Elevation	6300/ + 800, − 800
Navigation	Road
Time	Full day
Season	Late December through mid-April
USGS topo	15′ series, Tahoe
Start	In McKinney Estates off Highway 89 about 8 miles south of Tahoe City. From Tahoe Ski Bowl Way which is at the southern boundary of Homewood, drive 1.2 miles south to McKinney Rubicon Springs Road. Turn west (right) onto McKinney Rubicon Springs Road and drive 0.3 mile where you turn left onto Bellevue Avenue. Continue for 0.2 mile where you turn right onto Rubicon Avenue (Springs Court) and in another 0.3 mile turn left onto McKinney Rubicon Springs Road once again. In 0.1 mile you intersect Evergreen Way. This intersection is where the tour begins.

If you have reached the starting point of the tour, then you have overcome the only navigational problem. Now you can enjoy a pleasant tour through a very scenic area.

At the starting point, follow the snow-covered continuation of McKinney Rubicon Springs Road for 1.5 miles to McKinney Creek (**1**). Cross to the north side of the creek if there is sufficient snow to do so; if not, ski upstream or downstream to find a suitable spot.

Continue west on the road for 0.9 mile to a point above and to the north of McKinney Lake (**2**). Then ski another 0.9 mile to Lily Lake (**3**). Continue west on the road for another 0.6 mile to Miller Lake (**4**). In the past, the cabin marked on the topo at the north edge of Miller Lake made a nice shelter for lunch during cold, windy weather; regretfully it no longer exists.

From Miller Lake, continue west on the road for 0.3 mile to Miller Meadows which is the destination of this tour. The section from Lily Lake to Miller Meadows is flat, and you can ski across Lily and Miller Lakes if they are well-frozen.

You can reach Richardson Lake, located 0.9 mile to the south of Miller Meadows, by following the Richardson Lake tour.

30 Richardson Lake

MAP 16
PAGE 81

Difficulty	3
Length	10 miles round trip
Elevation	6300/ + 1100, − 1100
Navigation	Road and map
Time	Full day
Season	Late December through mid-April
USGS topo	15′ series, Tahoe
Start	In McKinney Estates off Highway 89 about 8 miles south of Tahoe City. Detailed directions are given in the Miller Meadows tour (no. 29).

Richardson Lake is a beautiful spot to relax and eat a leisurely lunch. Although, Richardson Lake is only a short distance from Miller Meadows, the extra mile increases the difficulty level because it requires navigation through dense woods.

Begin the tour to Richardson Lake by skiing the 4.2 miles to Miller Meadows **(5)** as described in that tour (no. 29). Between Miller Lake and Miller Meadows, there is a road heading south from the road you are on. You can reach Richardson Lake by following this road south for 0.9 mile; unfortunately it is a difficult road to spot or follow.

As an alternative to following the road, from the east end of Miller Meadows, ski south for 0.1 mile until you reach several old structures. From the structures, follow the creek which drains Richardson Lake for 0.7 mile to the lake. You can also follow a compass bearing to the lake.

Ludlow Hut, a Sierra Club cabin, is located at Richardson Lake. The hut, which was built in 1955, is located about 100 yards east of the lake and slightly above it; about where the "L" is in "Richardson Lake" on the 1955 topo. For reservations contact:

Clair Tappaan Lodge
P.O. Box 36
Norden, California 95724

Most skiers will choose to retrace their tracks to return. If you are more adventuresome, you can return to Highway 89 via General Creek. Refer to the McKinney Creek and General Creek Loop tour for details.

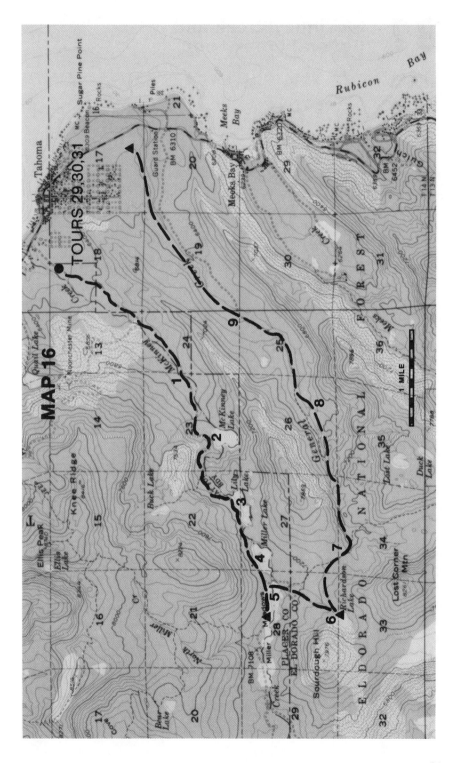

MAP 16

TOURS 29,30,31

31 McKinney Creek and General Creek Loop

MAP 16
PAGE 81

Difficulty	4
Length	12 miles one-way
Elevation	6300/ + 1100, − 1100
Navigation	Road, marked trail, map and compass
Time	Full day
Season	January through March
USGS topo	15′ series, Tahoe
Start	In McKinney Estates off Highway 89 about 8 miles south of Tahoe City. Detailed directions are given in the Miller Meadows tour (no. 29).
End	Ski touring trailhead in Sugar Pine Point State Park on Highway 89, 0.8 mile south of Tahoma.

This challenging tour covers the wide variety of terrain of both the Richardson Lake and General Creek tours and a more difficult section in the upper reaches of General Creek where you can expect slow going. You will feel a sense of accomplishment upon the completion of this tour.

Since the entire south side of the ridge dominated by Peak 7859 is subject to avalanches, ski this tour only when the snow is stable.

From the starting point, ski to Richardson Lake (6) by following the Richardson Lake tour (no. 30). From the lake, traverse through the trees and around the north ridge of Lost Corner Mountain to the very broad saddle (7) between Lost Corner Mountain and Peak 7859. A good reference point, Peak 7859, is occasionally visible to you as you traverse.

From the saddle, descend to General Creek along the route of the summer trail until you reach the creek which you cross to its south side in order to avoid a rock buttress of Peak 7859.

Continue to descend east along General Creek for 1.4 miles until you reach the creek from Duck Lake (8). The skiing in this last section is very difficult, and you can expect to spend one to two hours climbing over, around, up, and down boulders, trees, and cliffs.

When you reach the creek from Duck Lake, you may want to cross back to the north side of General Creek. Continue east along General Creek as the terrain rapidly opens up and the skiing becomes easier and more pleasurable for 1.3 miles until you intersect the General Creek marked ski touring trail (9) near where it crosses the creek. Now you simply follow the marked trail to the end of the tour. This last section is described in the General Creek tour (no. 33).

Ludlow Hut   Kim Grandfield

32 Sugar Pine Point State Park

MAP 17
PAGE 85

Difficulty	1
Length	Short
Elevation	6300/Nil
Navigation	Marked trail
Time	Few hours
Season	Late December through March
USGS topo	15' series, Tahoe; trail map available at trailhead
Start	Ski touring trailhead in Sugar Pine Point State Park on Highway 89, 0.8 mile south of Tahoma.

There are two very easy trails for beginners in Sugar Pine Point State Park; one is a loop in the campground area and the other is a loop on the east side of Highway 89 along the shore of Lake Tahoe. Both of these marked trails begin at the ski touring trailhead along with a longer, third tour which is also suitable for beginners. This longer tour is described in the General Creek tour.

Sugar Pine Point State Park is open all winter for camping. Hot water and heated restrooms are provided in the campground which is quiet during the winter months.

Breaking trail

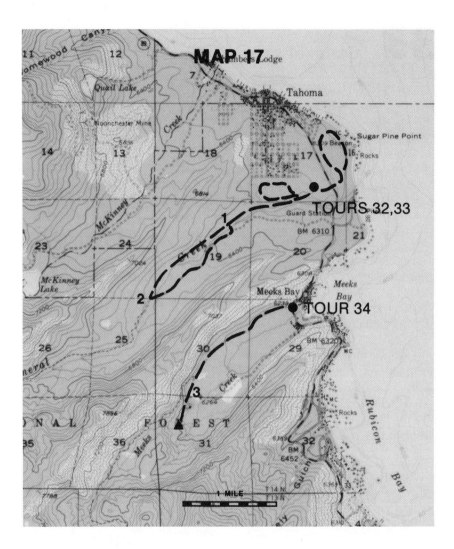

MAP 17

33 General Creek

MAP 17
PAGE 85

Difficulty	2
Length	4 miles round trip
Elevation	6300/ + 150, − 150
Navigation	Marked trail
Time	Half day
Season	Late December through March
USGS topo	15′ series, Tahoe; trail map available at trailhead
Start	Ski touring trailhead in Sugar Pine Point State Park on Highway 89, 0.8 mile south of Tahoma.

Away from the annoying highway and snowmobiles, this area is a very pleasant place to ski. Beginners planning to ski here should also read the Sugar Pine Point State Park tour description.

From the trailhead, follow the marked trail for 0.6 mile to a trail junction **(1)**. Continue to the southwest along the north side of General Creek for 1.5 miles until the marked trail crosses to the south side of the creek **(2)**. Now ski northeast for 1.5 miles until the marked trail crosses back to the north side of the creek where you return to the junction **(1)**. Complete the tour by following the trail back to the trailhead.

You can lengthen this tour by continuing southwest along General Creek past the turnaround point. For the first mile past the turnaround, the skiing is only a little more difficult; farther on, it becomes much more difficult.

Gentle climb

MAP **17**
PAGE 85

Meeks Creek **34**

Difficulty	1–2
Length	3 miles round trip
Elevation	6200/Nil
Navigation	Road
Time	Few hours
Season	Late December through March
USGS topo	15′ series, Tahoe
Start	Meeks Bay on Highway 89 about 12 miles south of Tahoe City and 17 miles north of the intersection of Highways 50 and 89 in South Lake Tahoe.

Meeks Creek is located in a heavily wooded valley through which you travel on a level and easy-to-follow road. This protected area is an excellent location to ski during a storm.

The tour begins at the building on the west side of the highway and on the north side of Meeks Creek, and follows the adjacent road. This road is also the beginning of the well-known Tahoe to Yosemite Trail.

From the highway, ski west on the road for 1.5 miles until it starts to climb **(3)**. You can extend the tour beyond this point by continuing on the road as it climbs 100′ in the next 0.2 mile to an abandoned cabin. Past the cabin, you can climb on the road for another 100′ in 0.3 mile until the valley comes to an abrupt end.

Late afternoon descent   *Gary Clark*

MAP 18
PAGE 90

35 Painted Rock Loop

Difficulty	3
Length	9 miles round trip
Elevation	6600/ + 1200, − 1200
Navigation	Road, marked trail and map
Time	Full day
Season	Mid-December through early April
USGS topo	15′ series, Tahoe; 7.5′ series, Kings Beach, Tahoe City
Start	North Tahoe High School. From the main intersection in Tahoe City, drive 2.8 miles northeast on North Lake Blvd. (Highway 28) to the Dollar Hill Shell Station. At the gas station turn left onto Fabian Way, drive for 0.1 mile and turn right onto Village Road. Drive another 0.2 mile and turn left onto Polaris Road and follow it for 0.7 mile to North Tahoe High School.

You should plan this tour for a clear day so you can enjoy the views of Lake Tahoe and the wide variety of ski touring terrain. This tour takes you on marked (groomed) trails, snow-covered roads, and steep slopes.

As you read the following description of the route, note that there are many road junctions. Take sufficient time to follow the description carefully in order to save a great deal of time in the end.

On this tour, you travel on Burton Creek State Park roads which have been groomed by Tahoe Nordic Ski Center. Ordinarily, you are expected to pay for skiing on them. However, according to the District Superintendent of the Department of Parks and Recreation, you can ski on them without paying a fee as long as the trails are on public land. Since this condition will prevail as long as skiers do not abuse the privilege, please abide by the following rules: do not ski on trails located on private property (all trails described in this tour are located in the public park or in the national forest); ski off the groomed track if you are headed in the direction opposite to traffic on the track.

Up to and including the winter of 1985, Tahoe Nordic marked road junctions with letters. The letters which were used in the winter of 1985 are indicated in parentheses, but realize that Tahoe Nordic may change them at any time.

Begin the tour by skiing west on the unplowed extension of Polaris Road for 0.2 mile until you reach a road junction (1). Shortly after starting, you pass the "Burton Creek State Park" sign marking the entrance.

At the junction, turn south (left) and ski on the road for 0.3 mile until the route and road turns northwest. Near this point, you may see another road heading northeast or another one heading south.

35

Take the road to the northwest and ski for 0.3 mile until you approach Burton Creek. Continue along the north side of the creek for 0.3 mile until you encounter a road junction (M) **(2)**. In the winter of 1985, the groomed tracks continued along the road to the north (right). On this tour, you want the road to the northwest (left) which parallels the creek.

Continue along the creek for 0.4 mile until you cross a small creek and then for 0.2 mile to a road junction (I) **(3)**. Take the road which heads north (right) until you reach another junction (F) **(4)** shortly thereafter.

Continue on the road to the northwest (left) and parallel to Burton Creek, which is out of sight, for 0.8 mile to another road junction (G) **(5)**. At this junction, you leave the creek and follow the road to the north (right) for 0.1 mile to yet another road junction (H) **(6)** where you finally leave the tracks of the nordic center.

At the junction, climb gradually on the road which heads west (left) for 0.3 mile until the road levels where, with careful observation, you can find an abandoned road **(7)** leading north (right) from the road you are on. From this junction, you now ski a loop which starts on the road to the north and returns on the road which continues west (straight).

Climb steadily for 0.5 mile on the abandoned road until it vanishes in a gully. Very early or late in the season, there is vegetation in the roadbed which should pose little difficulty. From the gully where the road vanishes, climb northwest at a very steep angle through trees to the saddle located on the ridge just north of Peak 7643. Once on the ridge, ski north for less than 0.1 mile to a well-defined road. At this excellent location to have lunch, you can enjoy the views of Lake Tahoe, Mt. Watson, Peak 7908, and Painted Rock.

Continue by skiing north (left) on the road for 0.1 mile to a fork **(8)**. The road to the northwest (right) leads to Starratt Pass; you want the road to the west (left) on which you descend gradually for 0.7 mile as it traverses below Peak 7908. When the road levels and turns south **(9)**, you can make a side trip up Painted Rock which you reach by a steep 350′ climb. Be sure to avoid the northern slopes of Painted Rock which are prone to avalanche.

To continue on the loop tour if you have climbed Painted Rock, return to the road. From the turn **(9)** in the road, descend on the road to the south which follows a drainage. Do not take the road which climbs to the south. After descending on the road for 0.9 mile, you reach a road junction **(10)**. Turn northeast (left) and follow the road as it weaves east for 0.5 mile until you reach the junction **(7)** with the abandoned road.

From the junction, simply retrace your route to the starting point. Since you are skiing in the opposite direction of the groomed trail traffic, remember to ski off the tracks.

MAP 18

TOURS 35, 36

1 MILE

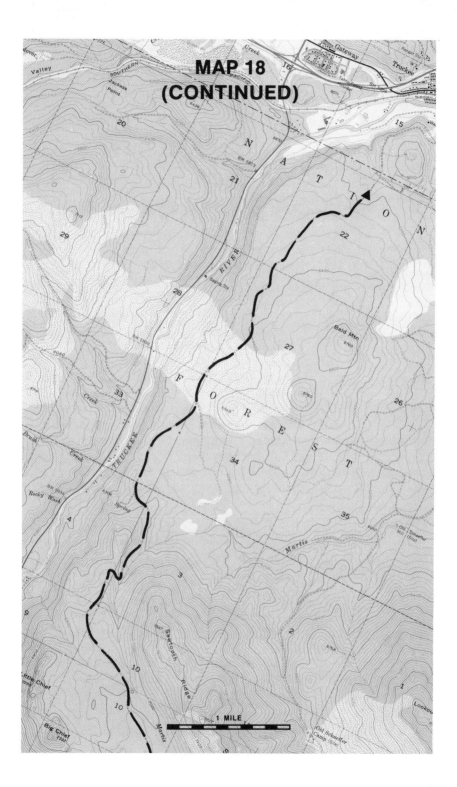

MAP 18
(CONTINUED)

1 MILE

36 Tahoe City to Truckee

MAP 18
PAGES 90–91

Difficulty	4
Length	15 miles one-way
Elevation	6600/+1450, −2200
Navigation	Road, marked trail, map and compass
Time	Full day
Season	Late December through March
USGS topo	15' series, Tahoe, Truckee; 7.5' series, Kings Beach, Tahoe City, Truckee
Start	North Tahoe High School. From the main intersection in Tahoe City, drive 2.8 miles northeast on North Lake Blvd. (Highway 28) to the Dollar Hill Shell Station. At the gas station turn left onto Fabian Way, drive for 0.1 mile and turn right onto Village Road. Drive another 0.2 mile and turn left onto Polaris Road and follow it for 0.7 mile to North Tahoe High School.
End	Ponderosa Palisades subdivision in Truckee. From the main intersection in downtown Truckee drive southeast for 0.5 mile on Highway 267 and turn right onto Palisades Road. Continue for 0.3 mile until the road curves right and in another 0.1 mile you are forced to make a left turn onto Ponderosa Drive. Drive for 0.5 mile and turn right onto Silver Fir Drive. Drive for 0.4 mile and turn left onto Thelin Drive. A gate on the right side of the road, 0.2 mile ahead, marks the ending point.

Except for a short distance near the start, the route of this tour is the same as The Great Ski Race, sponsored each year by Tahoe Nordic Ski Center. With the aid of a groomed track, racers have completed this course in less than two hours. Without the groomed trail, you may find the slower pace more desirable since it affords you countless opportunities to appreciate the spectacular views of Lake Tahoe, the high peaks to the west of the Truckee River, and the mountains to the north.

The first 2.9 miles of this tour are identical to the Painted Rock Loop tour (no. 35). Refer to that tour description for directions to the junction (7) with the abandoned road and for information about skiing on the groomed trails in the area.

From the junction, the abandoned road which heads north can be used to reach Starratt Pass as described in the Painted Rock Loop tour; this tour follows the main road and The Great Ski Race route west. Ski west for 0.4 until you cross a creek drainage and then for another 0.1 mile to a road junction **(10)**.

Take the north (right) fork, climb west, and then climb north for 0.9 mile until the road levels and turns east (right) **(9)**. Continue on the road as it traverses below Peak 7908 for 0.7 mile to a road junction **(8)**. Turn northwest (left) and ski on the road for 0.3 mile to Starratt Pass **(11)**.

At Starratt Pass, leave the road which continues northeast and descend to the north along the steep drainage for 0.7 mile to Deer Creek. From the creek, climb north for 0.1 mile and 100′ until you intersect a road **(12)**. In the drainage which you descended and elsewhere along this tour, you may see markers denoting the Truckee Sierra Skiway. It is believed that these markers first appeared in the 1960s as part of an industrious effort to mark a ski trail system in the Sierra.

Once you are on the road, follow it for 7.3 miles to the northwest and then north to the ending point. Because the road descends gradually or is level for most of the distance, you must pay close attention so you do not lose it. Use landmarks, such as Sawtooth Ridge, Martis Creek, Bald Mountain, and subtle changes in terrain to help you establish your location. You may also encounter some markers along the way but do not plan to rely on them.

Perfect spring touring

37 Brockway Summit to Agate Bay

MAP 19
PAGE 95

Difficulty	3
Length	2 miles one-way
Elevation	7200/ − 750
Navigation	Road
Time	Short
Season	Late December through March
USGS topo	15' series, Truckee, Tahoe; 7.5' series, Martis Peak, Kings Beach
Start	Just south of Brockway Summit on Highway 267. Park in the plowed area on the west side of the highway.
End	A housing development adjacent to Agate Bay. From North Lake Blvd., drive northwest on Agate Road for 0.4 mile to Tripoli Road. Turn right and drive 0.1 mile to the first road on your left. This is Old Wood Road or USFS Road 16N02. If you reach Granite Road you have gone too far. Even if it is possible to drive up Old Wood Road, it is best to park near its junction with Tripoli Road.

The entirely downhill run and the good views of Lake Tahoe are the highlights of this tour. Ski this short but steep tour if you want to liberate that final bit of energy which remains after completing one of the other tours in the Brockway Summit area and if you have powder snow. In the past, this route along USFS roads took skiers from the starting point to Carnelian Bay. Unfortunately, due to recent construction, the tour now terminates in the Agate Bay housing development.

Very close to the starting point is a radio tower and small building. You begin the tour by skiing southwest on Mt. Watson Road which is visible near the tower. Do not confuse this road with another one which descends to the south.

Follow Mt. Watson Road, which is level, for 0.3 mile to a road junction (1). The north (right) fork leads to Sawmill Flat and is part of the Brockway Summit to Tahoe City and Brockway Summit to Northstar tours. You want the south (left) fork which is Old Wood Road.

From the junction, descend on Old Wood Road for 0.6 mile until you pass snow-covered Regency Street (2) on your left. Continue to descend for 0.3 mile until you make a sharp left turn with the road. Ski another 0.4 mile on the road until it enters a housing development where the road is plowed. Either ski parallel to or walk on the road for 0.1 mile to Tripoli Road where the tour ends.

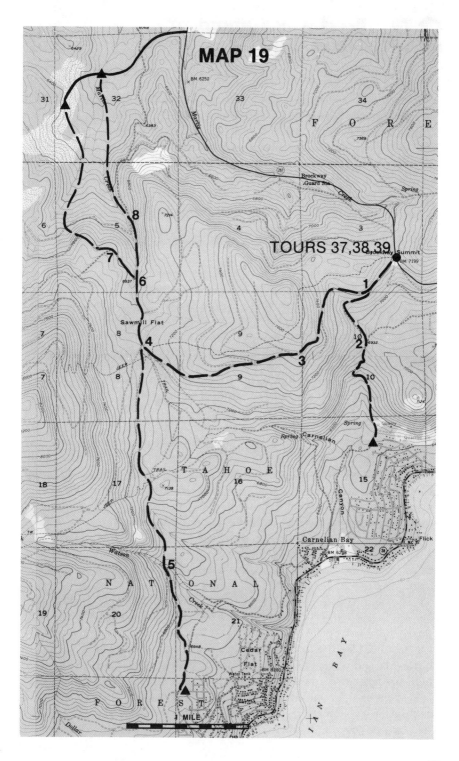

MAP 19

TOURS 37,38,39

MAP 19
PAGE 95

38 Brockway Summit to Tahoe City

Difficulty	3
Length	6 miles one-way
Elevation	7200/ + 250, − 750
Navigation	Road
Time	Up to most of a day
Season	Late December through March
USGS topo	15′ series, Truckee, Tahoe; 7.5′ series, Martis Peak, Kings Beach
Start	Just south of Brockway Summit on Highway 267. Park in the plowed area on the west side of the highway.
End	West end of Fulton Crescent in Cedar Flat. From the main intersection in Tahoe City, drive northeast on North Lake Blvd. (Highway 28) for 3.5 miles to Old Country Road. Turn north onto Old Country Road, drive for 0.7 miles, and turn right onto La Crosse Drive. At the tee intersection 0.3 mile ahead, turn left onto Fulton Crescent and drive 0.1 mile to its end.

Like the Brockway Summit to Agate Bay tour, this downhill run to Tahoe City offers excellent views of Lake Tahoe. Unlike the short tour to Agate Bay, this longer tour to Tahoe City seems to justify the extra effort of running a car shuttle.

At the starting point, locate Mt. Watson Road near the radio tower and small building. Do not confuse it with the road that descends to the south. Ski southwest on Mt. Watson Road, which is level, for 0.3 mile to a junction (1). Continue on the north (right) fork for 0.6 mile until you pass a road on your left. Ski for 0.3 mile to an obvious vista point and high point of the road (3) where the view of Lake Tahoe is superb.

Continue to follow Mt. Watson Road west for 1.5 miles to Sawmill Flat (4). As you encounter the several road junctions along this last section, always follow Mt. Watson Road, the main road, which heads west and downhill. When Mt. Watson Road becomes level, several roads intersect and head south. The first one is USFS Road 16N48, 0.1 mile farther west is another, and still 0.1 mile farther west is a major junction at Sawmill Flat.

At Sawmill Flat, the road to the north heads downhill towards Northstar Ski Resort and is described in the Brockway Summit to Northstar tour. There are also two roads which head south. Of these, the westernmost (right) road is the continuation of Mt. Watson Road; do not follow it. You want the easternmost (left) of the two which is a Forest Service Protection Road that intersects Mt. Watson Road just past the road to Northstar. Be aware that at least one previous road and other subsequent roads are marked as Forest Service Protection Roads.

Ski south on the easternmost (left) road for 1.8 miles until you reach Watson Creek (**5**). After the first level 1.1 miles, the road descends steadily. Just past the creek, you pass a road on your right. Continue to descend for 0.3 mile until you pass a road on your left and for a short distance farther until you pass a road on your right.

Continue south for 0.2 mile until several roads come together. Keep to the right and continue skiing south for 0.2 mile until the road becomes very level. Ski for 0.2 mile until you reach Fulton Crescent and the end of the tour on the east (left) side of the road. As you approach Fulton Crescent, you can see houses on the east side of the road.

Lake Tahoe from Mt. Watson Road

MAP **19**
PAGE 95

39 **Brockway Summit to Northstar**

Difficulty	3
Length	5 miles one-way
Elevation	7200/+150, −1250
Navigation	Road and map
Time	Half day
Season	December through mid-April
USGS topo	15′ series, Truckee, Tahoe; 7.5′ series, Martis Peak, Kings Beach
Start	Just south of Brockway Summit on Highway 267. Park in the plowed area on the west side of the highway.
End	Lodge at Northstar Ski Resort or at West Martis Creek. From Highway 267 drive 0.8 towards Northstar Ski Resort to West Martis Creek. Park on the south side of the road just east of the creek. Some trash containers and a sign indicating stables may be your best landmarks. To reach the ski resort continue on the road for 0.4 mile.

This tour offers the same wonderful views of Lake Tahoe as the Brockway Summit to Tahoe City tour. You can end this tour either at Northstar Ski Resort or at West Martis Creek. Of the two, the tour ending at West Martis Creek is more difficult due to the final 1.2 miles through dense trees.

Begin the tour by skiing 2.7 miles to Sawmill Flat (**4**) as described in the Brockway Summit to Tahoe City tour (no. 38). At the flat, locate the road that descends north toward Northstar and follow it for 0.6 mile to a dam (**6**) not shown on the topo. Do not attempt to ski on the reservoir since the ice is never stable.

Ski to the base of the north side of the dam directly or by following the road as it loops down to the base. When you are at the base of the dam, find the roads heading in two directions.

To reach Northstar Ski Resort. To reach the lodge at Northstar Ski Resort, follow the road which crosses West Martis Creek at the base of the dam. Climb gradually for 0.3 mile to a road junction (**7**). Continue on the north (right) fork for 0.4 mile to the downhill ski slopes just above the day lodge. Ski down to the day lodge and then follow the easy runs to the main lodge area.

To reach West Martis Creek. To reach the ending point on West Martis Creek from the base of the dam, follow the road to the north and parallel the creek on its east side for 0.5 mile to a plowed road (**8**). This private road leads to Northstar's maintenance area and cannot be used for an ending point. To continue, cross the plowed road, descend to West Martis Creek, and then ski north along the creek for 1.2 miles to the ending point.

Lunch with a view

40 Martis Peak

MAP 20
PAGE 101

Difficulty	3
Length	7 miles round trip
Elevation	7100/ + 1650, − 1650
Navigation	Road and map
Time	Full day
Season	December through April
USGS topo	15′ series, Truckee; 7.5′ series, Martis Peak
Start	Highway 267, 0.5 mile north of Brockway Summit. Park in the plowed area on the east side of the road where the highway makes a sharp turn.

Ski to the top of Martis Peak if you want unbeatable views of Lake Tahoe. Do this tour immediately after a new snowfall when you can enjoy a thrilling descent.

From the highway, climb steadily east on the snow-covered road for 1.1 mile until you reach a road junction (1). In this first section, expect to pass several small roads as you continue on the obvious main road.

At the road junction, USFS Road 16N33 descends east (straight); instead take the road which turns north (left) and ski for 0.5 mile to a large flat area (2) where several roads connect and a drainage descends southeast. Climb steadily on the road which heads northeast for 1.3 miles to the south ridge (3) of Martis Peak. If you see any forks in the road while ascending, always continue up and to the northeast.

At the south ridge of Martis Peak, a road turns north (left) off the one you have been on. If you can see the road to the north, you can ski on it for 0.6 mile to a fire lookout and then climb 0.1 mile southeast to the Martis Peak summit. If you cannot see the road, ski for 0.6 mile along the ridge top to the summit. At the summit, savor both the glorious views and those tasty morsels you carried up.

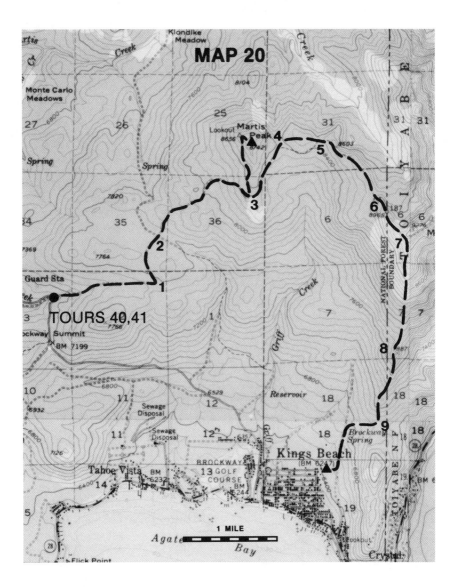

MAP 20

41 Martis Peak and Mt. Baldy Traverse

MAP 20
PAGE 101

Difficulty	5
Length	9 miles one-way
Elevation	7100/+2200, −2800
Navigation	Road, map and compass
Time	Full day
Season	Late December through early April
USGS topo	15' series, Truckee, Mt. Rose, Tahoe; 7.5' series, Martis Peak, Mt. Rose, Kings Beach
Start	Highway 267, 0.5 mile north of Brockway Summit. Park in the plowed area on the east side of the road where the highway makes a sharp turn.
End	Corner of Speckled Street and Chipmunk Street in Kings Beach. Speckled Street intersects Highway 267 3.0 miles southeast of Brockway Summit and 0.3 mile north of North Lake Blvd. (Highway 28) in Kings Beach. Drive 0.8 mile east on Speckled Street to the dead end at Chipmunk Street.

This advanced tour, which offers spectacular views, solitude, and lots of downhill, challenges even the most advanced cross-country skier. The route climbs from Brockway Summit to the saddle just east of Martis Peak, then makes a giant traverse along a ridge to Mt. Baldy, and finally drops 2500' to Kings Beach. The route described below does not actually pass over Martis Peak or Mt. Baldy although both can be climbed along the way.

Begin this tour by following the Martis Peak tour (no. 40) for 2.9 miles to the south ridge (3) of the peak. Continue on the road which traverses northeast to the saddle (4) east of the peak.

As an alternative, you can ascend the south ridge of Martis Peak to the summit and then descend east to the saddle. This excursion adds only 0.3 mile but 400' of climbing.

From the saddle, climb east for 0.3 mile to the top of a small knob. Then descend east for 0.1 mile to a saddle (5) where you have views to the north of several reservoirs. Now climb to the east for 0.2 mile to Peak 8603 which is at the northwest end of a narrow ridge which parallels the upper reaches of Juniper Creek.

From Peak 8603, ski southeast along the ridge where a view of Lake Tahoe to the south awaits you. As you continue southeast, stay close to the ridge no matter how advantageous dropping down may seem. If you drop too low, you will have a steeper than necessary climb, or you will end up in an avalanche area southwest of Mt. Baldy.

41

At a point **(6)** just west of the California-Nevada border, you climb southeast at a very steep angle along the ridge and then gradually to the south ridge **(7)** of Mt. Baldy. When you reach the obvious south ridge, the summit of Mt. Baldy will be 0.1 mile to the northeast and 100′ above.

Looking south and down the ridge you can see Kings Beach and the knob on the ridge just to the east (left) of the town toward which the route heads. You can also see Agate Bay and Crystal Bay respectively on the west and east sides of Stateline Point.

Descend gradually south along the ridge for 0.2 mile and enjoy the open terrain which is perfect for touring. As you descend, enjoy the views of Truckee, Donner Lake, Martis Peak and the section you traversed earlier. Also, if you look very carefully south, you can see overhead cables, which you will encounter later, crossing the ridge.

As you begin to drop at a steeper angle, be aware of avalanche danger even though you are technically on a ridge. As you descend to Peak 7887 **(8)**, the terrain remains quite open. You pass the peak on its west (right), then continue south, and descend into the trees. If necessary, use a compass to stay on the ridge.

Ski through the trees until you reach a saddle. From the saddle, traverse south around the west (right) side of a small knob. From the south side of the knob, descend south for a short distance to a clearing **(9)** where the previously mentioned overhead cables cross the ridge.

From the ridge, follow the cables west and down the clearing. Part way down the clearing, you may see a road heading south; do not follow it. Instead continue west and down to a road where the cables turn south (left). Follow the road as it parallels the cables.

Ski south on the road for 0.1 mile to a fork. The cables follow the east (left) fork; you should continue on the west (right) fork for 0.5 mile until the cables cross the road you are on. At the cables, turn west (right) and follow them for 0.1 mile to the ending point of the tour.

Fire lookout near Martis Peak

MAP 21
PAGE 107

Northstar to Lake Tahoe via Mt. Pluto 42

Difficulty	4
Length	7 miles one-way
Elevation	6400/ + 2200, − 1900
Navigation	Map and compass
Time	Full day
Season	Late December through March
USGS topo	15′ series, Truckee, Tahoe
Start	Northstar Ski Resort located off Highway 267 between Truckee and Kings Beach.
End	West end of Fulton Crescent in Cedar Flat. From the main intersection in Tahoe City, drive northeast on North Lake Blvd. (Highway 28) for 3.5 miles to Old Country Road. Turn north onto Old Country Road, drive for 0.7 miles, and turn right onto La Crosse Drive. At the tee intersection 0.3 mile ahead, turn left onto Fulton Crescent and drive 0.1 mile to its end.

The main attraction of this tour is the 1900′ descent from the summit of Mt. Pluto to Lake Tahoe. The price you pay for the downhill run is a steep 2200′ climb from the base of Northstar Ski Resort to the summit of Mt. Pluto.

If you are seeking ideal downhill conditions for the descent, I recommend early spring when the corn-snow can be excellent all the way down to Lake Tahoe. The tour is even better with powder snow, but you will rarely find good powder all the way down to the lake.

To reach the summit of Mt. Pluto, simply follow but stay off the groomed ski slopes at Northstar. From Northstar Village, first follow the Big Springs chairlift to the day lodge. From the day lodge, follow the Aspen chairlift to the base of the Comstock chairlift. Next climb west at a steep angle for 0.3 mile, following a ski run, not a chairlift, to the north ridge of Mt. Pluto. Northstar refers to this ridge as the West Ridge run. Once you are on the ridge, you climb south along it to the summit of Mt. Pluto (1).

From the summit of Mt. Pluto, descend east on a road for 0.5 mile to the top of the Rendezvous chairlift (2). At the chairlift, leave the road and the hectic alpine ski scene and descend over the best downhill terrain of the tour to the southwest for 1.2 miles to the saddle (3) between Mt. Pluto and Mt. Watson. Savor the descent and take time to enjoy the views of Lake Tahoe as you descend through the scattered timber. Expect to cross several roads on your descent, following them only if they head in the correct direction.

From the saddle, traverse the northern slopes of Mt. Watson in a south-

105

easterly direction. If you find it, there is a road which you can follow around Watson Lake. From a point southeast of the lake where the road begins to descend, you leave the road and traverse east to the east ridge of Mt. Watson and to a broad saddle **(4)**.

From the broad saddle, ski to the southeast through several clearings and sparsely wooded areas until you reach a gully north of a ridge. Descend the gully until the terrain becomes level and continue east for 0.2 mile to the ending point at Fulton Crescent.

Ascending south ridge of Martis Peak

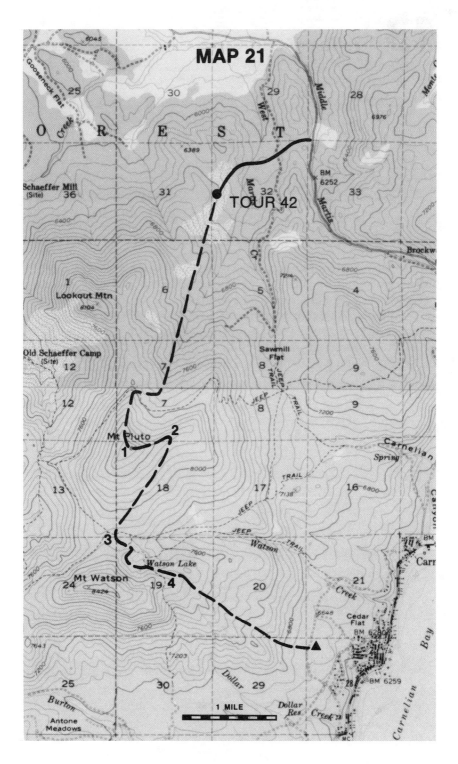

MAP 21

TOUR 42

107

43 Tahoe Meadows

MAP 22
PAGE 108

Difficulty	1
Length	Short
Elevation	8600/Nil
Navigation	Adjacent to road
Time	Short
Season	Late November through April
USGS topo	15' series, Mt. Rose
Start	Highway 431 (formerly 27), 6.8 miles north of Highway 28 and Incline Village, and 1.4 miles south of Mt. Rose Summit.

The relatively high altitude and the lack of vegetation make Tahoe Meadows a good choice for skiing very early in the season. The large, flat, open meadows, and the bordering mild hills offer plenty of easy touring and the best opportunities for beginners to learn new techniques. Across the highway and next to the road are steeper slopes for the more adventuresome. While touring in this area, keep in mind that all the slopes in the Mt. Rose area should be considered avalanche prone.

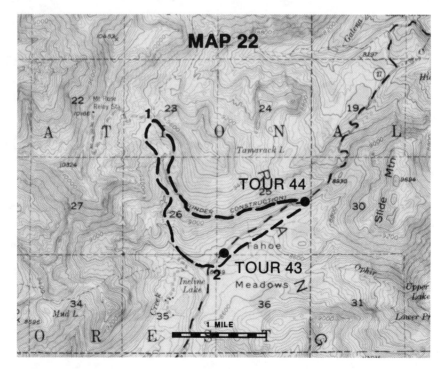

MAP 22

MAP 22
PAGE 108

Third Creek Loop 44

Difficulty	3
Length	6 miles round trip
Elevation	8850/ + 900, − 900
Navigation	Road and map
Time	Half day
Season	December through April
USGS topo	15′ series, Mt. Rose
Start	Highway 431 (formerly 27), 7.9 miles north of Highway 28 and Incline Village, and 0.3 mile south of Mt. Rose Summit. A road and building are located on the north side of the highway.

Ski touring in the Mt. Rose area has good and bad points. Its high altitude location makes it a good choice for anxious tourers who want to ski at the first falling of snow. If you belong to this category of skiers, you should also consider the Tahoe Meadows tour. Unfortunately, cold, windy weather plagues this rugged area where navigation is difficult, avalanche danger is considerable, and good ski touring terrain is limited. Regardless of these conditions, the loop described below offers good intermediate terrain.

From the highway, ski west on the snow-covered road as it gradually turns north into a canyon for 2.4 miles until you reach a saddle (1), the highest point of the tour. Mt. Rose with its steep slopes is to the north, and beyond here the road continues across very steep and dangerous terrain to the Mt. Rose Relay Station.

The return trip from the saddle is along Third Creek. Descend south along the creek for 1.5 miles and then turn east (there is no landmark) so that you intersect the highway (2) at the southwest end of Tahoe Meadows.

Complete the loop by skiing gradually uphill along the south side of the highway to the starting point. Most of this final stretch is through Tahoe Meadows.

Following a backcountry track

South Tahoe

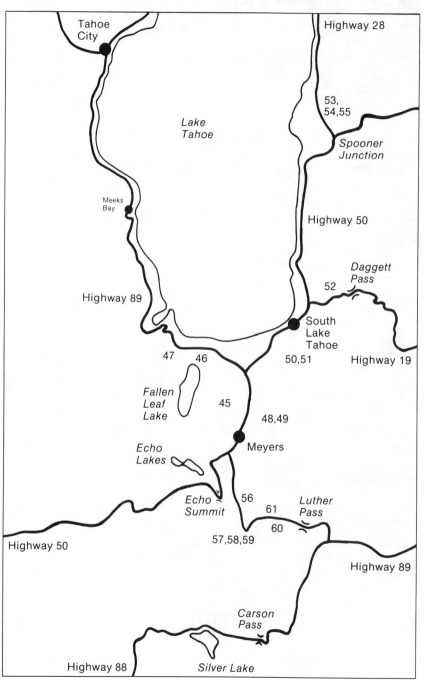

Tahoe City

Highway 28

53, 54, 55

Spooner Junction

Lake Tahoe

Meeks Bay

Highway 50

Daggett Pass

52

Highway 89

South Lake Tahoe

47   46

50,51

Highway 19

Fallen Leaf Lake

45

48,49

Echo Lakes

Meyers

Echo Summit

56

Luther Pass

61

60

57,58,59

Highway 50

Highway 89

Carson Pass

Highway 88

Silver Lake

Difficulty	3
Length	4 miles round trip to the lookout and 7 miles round trip to the lakes
Elevation	6700/+650, −650 to the lookout and 6700/+1000, −1000 to the lakes
Navigation	Road
Time	Half to most of a day
Season	Mid-December through mid-April
USGS topo	15′ series, Fallen Leaf Lake
Start	From the intersection of Highways 50 and 89 in South Lake Tahoe, drive southwest on Lake Tahoe Blvd. for 2.7 miles and turn right onto Tahoe Mountain Road. Drive 1.1 miles and turn right onto Glenmore Way and then immediately left onto Dundee Circle. In 0.1 mile turn left onto Tahoe Mountain Road once again and park. Do not drive down the narrow plowed portion of Tahoe Mountain Road which is just ahead.

Of the spectacular panorama from Angora Lookout, the most striking feature is the rich blue color of Fallen Leaf Lake and Lake Tahoe. Other impressive sights include: the Carson Range to the east and southeast; Mt. Tallac with its steep eastern slopes to the northwest; and Lake Valley to the southeast and below.

Start the tour by walking down Tahoe Mountain Road for 0.1 mile to a small meadow (1) on the left side of the road, which may be partially obscured by trees. Locate the snow-covered road which skirts the west (right) side of the meadow. Ski southwest on this level road for 0.5 mile and then for another 1.2 miles as it climbs steadily to a ridge top and Angora Lookout (2).

To continue to Angora Lakes, continue southwest on the ridge and road for 0.7 mile until the road begins to drop. Follow the road as it drops 150′ and then climbs 200′ in 0.9 mile to the lakes. If the road becomes too difficult to follow at its lowest point, head south and follow the power lines to the lakes. Be aware that skiing beneath the steep cliffs which descend from Angora and Echo Peaks to the upper lake is unsafe.

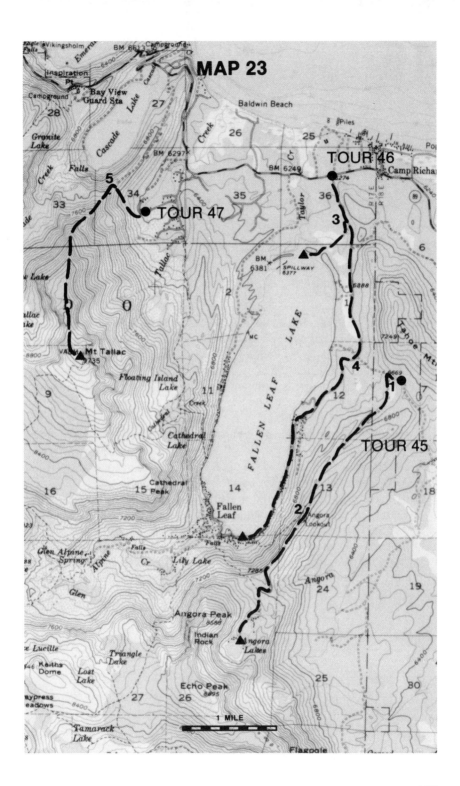

MAP 23

46 Fallen Leaf Lake

MAP 23
PAGE 113

Difficulty	1–2
Length	2 to 9 miles round trip
Elevation	6300/ + 100, – 100 to north end of lake or 6300/ + 400, – 400 to south end of lake
Navigation	Road and map
Time	Few hours to full day
Season	Late December through March
USGS topo	15′ series, Fallen Leaf Lake
Start	Intersection of Fallen Leaf Lake Road and Highway 89, 3.0 miles northwest of the intersection of Highways 50 and 89 in South Lake Tahoe, and 0.5 mile west of Camp Richardson.

No matter how far you choose to ski on Fallen Leaf Lake Road, the tour to Fallen Leaf Lake is an easy one. Created by glacial movement, the three-mile-long lake offers beginners the opportunity to ski all day without the anxiety of significant elevation changes.

Fallen Leaf Lake Road is subject to extreme variations in snow conditions due to its low elevation and its use by snowmobilers. Pick a time when the snow cover is good.

From Highway 89, ski south on Fallen Leaf Lake Road for 0.5 mile to a road junction **(3)**. The shortest route to the lake takes the west (right) fork which enters Fallen Leaf Campground. The longer route takes the east (left) fork which heads around the east side of the lake.

Short route. Follow the road into the campground for 0.3 mile until you reach the edge of a large meadow. At the meadow, leave the road and ski southwest (left) over a small rise to the lake.

Long route. From the junction **(3)**, you ski south on Fallen Leaf Lake Road for 1.5 miles until you pass Tahoe Mountain Road **(4)** on your left. Continue south on the road for another 2.6 miles to the south end of the lake. You can extend the tour by skiing on roads for 1.0 mile to Lily Lake.

MAP 23
PAGE 113

Mt. Tallac 47

Difficulty	5
Length	5 miles round trip
Elevation	6400/+3300, −3300
Navigation	Map
Time	Full day
Season	March and April
USGS topo	15′ series, Fallen Leaf Lake
Start	From the intersection of Highways 50 and 89 in South Lake Tahoe, drive 4.9 miles northwest on Highway 89 to Spring Creek Road and turn southwest onto it. Drive 0.4 mile, turn right onto Mattole Road, and continue for 0.4 mile to the starting point. You will need to park earlier if the road conditions are poor.

The satisfaction of meeting the challenge and an unparalleled view of Lake Tahoe, Desolation Wilderness and the Crystal Range are the rewards of this extremely demanding ascent of Mt. Tallac. Although the total distance is short, this very steep tour requires an early start.

From the starting point on Mattole Road, climb northwest to the north ridge (5) of Mt. Tallac where you can see Cascade Lake to the north. Once on the ridge, you follow it south to the summit of Mt. Tallac which becomes obvious as you approach the final slope. Since this slope as well as the bowls to the northeast of the summit are severely avalanche prone, this tour should not be attempted when conditions are unstable.

Lake Tahoe

MAP 24
PAGE 118

Fountain Place **48**

Difficulty	3
Length	9 miles round trip
Elevation	6300/ + 1500, − 1500
Navigation	Road
Time	Full day
Season	Late December through early April
USGS topo	15′ series, Freel Peak
Start	Corner of Oneidas Street and Chibcha in Meyers. From Highway 50 in Meyers follow Pioneer Trail northeast for 0.9 mile. Turn right onto Oneidas Street and Chibcha is 0.2 mile ahead.

The tour to Fountain Place allows you to ski all day without the worry of navigating because it follows roads the entire way. At Fountain Place, the meadow is a perfect setting for lunch. Freel Peak, the highest peak in the Tahoe Basin, is nearby to the east.

From the starting point, follow the snow-covered continuation of Oneidas Street for 0.6 mile to a road junction **(1)** where you take the fork to the east (right) and immediately intersect Saxon Creek. Cross the creek on the bridge and ski 1.7 miles on the road to another road junction **(2)**. Take the east (left) fork and ski for 0.1 mile where you cross Trout Creek on a bridge.

Continue on the road for 0.3 mile until you make a 180 degree right turn with it. Ahead, you ascend on the road at a steep angle for 0.9 mile. In this section, exercise caution immediately after heavy snowfalls and when other avalanche conditions exist. Continue on the road as it climbs gradually for another 0.9 mile to Fountain Place and the large meadow beyond.

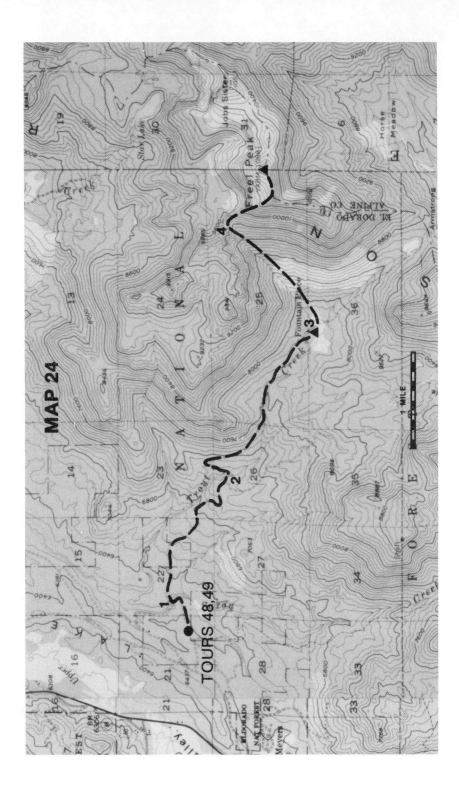

MAP 24

TOURS 48, 49

118

MAP 24
PAGE 118

Freel Peak 49

Difficulty	5
Length	14 miles round trip
Elevation	6300/+4600, −4600
Navigation	Road and map
Time	Very long day
Season	March and April
USGS topo	15' series, Freel Peak
Start	Corner of Oneidas Street and Chibcha in Meyers. From Highway 50 in Meyers follow Pioneer Trail northeast for 0.9 mile. Turn right onto Oneidas Street and Chibcha is 0.2 mile ahead.

The view from Freel Peak, the highest point in the Tahoe area, is dramatic. This extremely demanding one-day tour should be attempted by only the very strongest skiers. Since the avalanche danger on this tour is extreme, do not attempt this tour after a heavy snowfall or when other unstable conditions exist.

Begin the tour by skiing 4.6 miles to the meadow (3) adjacent to Fountain Place as described in that tour (no. 48). From the meadow, climb up a gully to the northeast for 1.4 miles and 1700' to the saddle (4) between Freel Peak and Peak 9885. This saddle separates Fountain Place and High Meadows.

From the saddle, climb southeast up a ridge to an east-west ridge of which Freel Peak is a part. Finally, ski east to the summit next to the microwave station.

50 High Meadows

MAP 25
PAGE 121

Difficulty	3
Length	7 miles round trip
Elevation	6550/+1400, −1400
Navigation	Road
Time	Most of a day
Season	Late December through early April
USGS topo	15′ series, Freel Peak
Start	End of High Meadows Trail in South Lake Tahoe. High Meadows Trail intersects Pioneer Trail 4.8 miles north of Highway 50 in Meyers and 2.6 miles south of Ski Run Blvd. in South Lake Tahoe. The end of High Meadows Trail is 0.8 mile south of Pioneer Trail.

This tour climbs steadily to a high point overlooking the basin in which High Meadows is located. Along part of the route there are good views of the mountains to the northwest.

From the starting point, ski east on the snow-covered road for 0.9 mile until you reach a locked gate (1) where a sign reads: "Be a good neighbor. Respect the land. Pack it in—pack it out. Private property. No vehicles. Trimmer Cattle Ranch." From this sign and given that the caretaker has not indicated that cross-country skiers are unwelcome, it appears to be okay for skiers to proceed. Look for a low section of fence which you can easily step over without damaging and respect all requests of the owner or caretaker.

Continue on the road, climbing for 0.4 mile and then descending for 0.1 mile, to a creek which you must cross carefully. Now the road becomes steeper, and you climb for 0.5 mile until you reach some power lines.

Just ahead is a fork in the road; take the north (left) fork and continue to climb on the road for 0.8 mile to the open high point (2) above High Meadows. If you lose the road as you are climbing, pick your own route to the east until you intersect the high point.

From the high point, the easiest route to the meadows is to turn north (left) and follow a level and open course until you reach the power lines again. Descend along the power lines to the north end of the meadows.

On your return trip, you may want to leave the road to enjoy a descent on the sparsely wooded terrain just below the high point. Farther down, if the descent on the fast road becomes too difficult, ski off and parallel to it.

MAP 25

TOURS 50,51

Climbing Mt. Tallac

Kim Grandfield

51 Star Lake

MAP 25
PAGE 121

Difficulty	5
Length	10 miles round trip
Elevation	6550/+2550, −2550
Navigation	Road, map and compass
Time	Full day
Season	Late December through early April
USGS topo	15′ series, Freel Peak
Start	End of High Meadows Trail in South Lake Tahoe. High Meadows Trail intersects Pioneer Trail 4.8 miles north of Highway 50 in Meyers and 2.6 miles south of Ski Run Blvd. in South Lake Tahoe. The end of High Meadows Trail is 0.8 mile south of Pioneer Trail.

On this tour to Star Lake, located at the base of and 1700′ below Jobs Sister, expect a steep climb and a wonderful descent. Before you begin, keep in mind that this tour traverses along many steep, potentially dangerous slopes, that the route-finding can be tricky, and that snow conditions improve as you go higher.

Begin the tour to Star Lake by following the High Meadows tour (no. 50) to the high point (2) above the meadows. Ski south along the ridge until you intersect a road. Weave south on the road for 0.9 mile until you climb at a very steep angle for 50 yards. Continue on the road for 0.1 mile until you intersect a creek (3).

At the creek, leave the road and ascend parallel to and on either side of the creek for 0.6 mile to an open area (4). From the open area, climb east toward the creek which drains Star Lake and then follow the creek to the lake. The lake is 0.5 mile from the open area.

MAP 26
PAGES 126–127

Kingsbury Grade to Spooner Junction

52

Difficulty	4
Length	10 miles one-way
Elevation	7600/ + 1100, − 1700
Navigation	Road, map and compass
Time	Full day
Season	Late December through mid-April
USGS topo	15′ series, Freel Peak, Carson City
Start	End of Andria Drive in Chalet Village. From South Lake Tahoe, drive east on Highway 19 (Kingsbury Grade) for 3.0 miles and turn north onto North Benjamin Drive. North Benjamin Drive turns into Andria Drive and 1.9 miles from the highway the plowed road ends.
End	Spooner Junction Maintenance Station, 0.3 mile south of the junction of Highways 50 and 28.

Although snowmobilers frequent the first half, this tour offers a sense of remoteness and fantastic views of Lake Tahoe to the west, Jacks Valley to the east, and beautiful high peaks.

The tour from Kingsbury Grade to Spooner Junction follows a true north course the entire way except for the final 1.5 mile run down to the maintenance station. Most of the route is marked with yellow diamonds.

Start the tour by climbing north at a steep angle on the snow-covered road for 0.3 mile to a road junction not shown on the topo. Follow the fork which makes a sharp turn to the west (left) and climb for 0.1 mile until you pass the turnoff (1) to Castle Rock on your left. As you climb, enjoy views of the higher peaks of the Tahoe Basin: East and Monument Peaks, Jobs Sister, and Jobs Peak. You can also see the cuts of the Heavenly Valley ski runs.

From the turnoff, continue north on the road for 0.6 mile until you reach a small saddle between Peaks 8204 and 8384. From the saddle, ski 0.4 mile until you pass a road (2) on your left which heads to the west and is not shown on the topo. In this 0.4 mile section, enjoy the beautiful views to the west of Lake Tahoe and beyond of Mt. Tallac and Pyramid Peak bordering Desolation Valley.

From the road you passed, continue north on the same road for 0.5 mile until it disappears. Traverse north for 1.2 miles until you are northwest of Peak 8863 where you get onto Genoa Peak Road (3), located in a gully.

Continue to the north for 0.5 mile until you pass Sierra Canyon which descends to the east. In the next section of gentle terrain, the road may be difficult to see, but you can simply continue north for 0.9 mile to the saddle (4) between Genoa and South Camp Peaks. Again continue north on the road, if possible, for 0.8 mile to a point **(5)** very close to the highest summit of South Camp Peak. While the top of South Camp Peak is slightly off the route, the summit is easy to reach and is a perfect lunch spot to enjoy the good views to the east.

If you are not on the road, you must locate it now. From directly east of South Camp Peak's highest summit, descend east into the trees and look for yellow diamond markers and the road cut. Once you find the road, you should have no trouble following it for the remainder of the tour.

Descend gradually north on the road until you pass a road **(6)** on your right which is 2.3 miles from South Camp Peak's highest summit. Follow the road as it turns west for 0.3 mile to a saddle located to the northeast of Peak 7819.

From the saddle, descend to the northwest on the road at a steep angle for 0.6 mile until you pass a road on your right. Then descend another 0.9 mile to the Spooner Junction Maintenance Station.

Star Lake

MAP 26
PAGE 127

North Canyon Creek 53

Difficulty	1
Length	2 miles round trip
Elevation	7000/Nil
Navigation	Road and marked trail
Time	Few hours
Season	December through early April
USGS topo	15' series, Carson City; trail map available at trailhead
Start	Lake Tahoe Nevada State Park on the east side of Highway 28, 0.7 mile north of Spooner Junction. A fee is charged for use of the park.

This area is a perfect place for beginners to start their ski touring career. Two beginner tours, North Canyon Creek and Spooner Lake, and one intermediate tour, Marlette Lake, are located in the park. The trails in the park are easy to follow and marked where necessary.

From the trailhead, descend east for 75 yards until you reach a road at the edge of a meadow and Spooner Lake. Ski north (left) on the road for 0.1 mile until you reach marker number "2" adjacent to the narrow clearing (**7**) which connects two large meadows. From this point, ski north across the narrow clearing and continue north on the road which parallels North Canyon Creek for 0.5 mile to two old buildings. Continue on the road for 0.1 mile until the road crosses the creek (**8**).

After crossing the creek, the road continues up North Canyon to Marlette Lake. Instead you leave the road and head south through trees and along the west side of North Canyon Creek for 0.4 mile until you reach the meadow. Cross the meadow to the south and enter the trees where you intersect a snow-covered road. Follow this road east (left) for 0.3 mile until you reach marker number "2" at the narrow clearing (**7**) you crossed earlier. Finally, retrace your tracks to the trailhead.

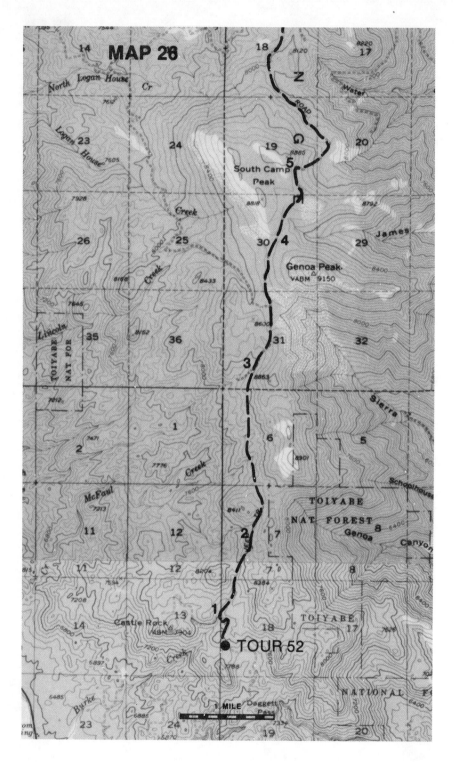

MAP 26

TOUR 52

126

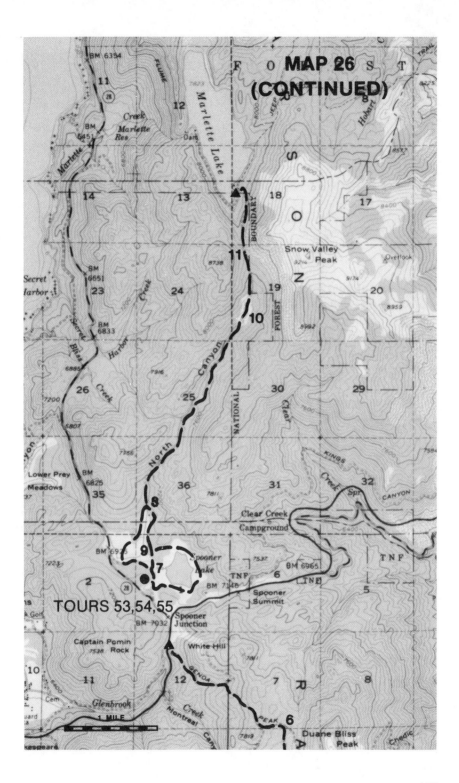

TOURS 53,54,55

54 Spooner Lake

MAP 26
PAGE 127

Difficulty	1
Length	2 miles round trip
Elevation	7000/Nil
Navigation	Marked trail
Time	Few hours
Season	December through early April
USGS topo	15' series, Carson City; trail map available at trailhead
Start	Lake Tahoe Nevada State Park on the east side of Highway 28, 0.7 mile north of Spooner Junction. A fee is charged for use of the park.

This tour around Spooner Lake is adjacent to the North Canyon Creek tour, and beginners can easily ski both in one day. The trail is usually well-tracked and is marked where necessary.

More advanced skiers may also enjoy this tour because it gives them the opportunity to kick up their heels and practice the diagonal stride on a fast track.

From the trailhead, descend east for 75 yards to the edge of a meadow and Spooner Lake where you intersect a road. Ski south (right) on the road for 75 yards to marker number "1". Turn east (left) and ski counterclockwise around Spooner Lake along the edge of the meadow. It is not safe to ski on the lake.

Ski for 1.2 miles until you reach the north side of the lake where you enter the trees, climb west over a gradual rise, and drop down to a road and marker number "3" **(9)**. Follow this road south (left) for 0.2 mile to a road junction and marker number "2" **(7)**. Then continue south (left) for 0.1 mile until you reach the point where you started the loop. Now simply climb back to the trailhead.

MAP 26
PAGE 127

Marlette Lake 55

Difficulty	3
Length	10 miles round trip
Elevation	7000/+1600, −1600
Navigation	Road
Time	Full day
Season	December through early April
USGS topo	15′ series, Carson City
Start	Lake Tahoe Nevada State Park on the east side of Highway 28, 0.7 mile north of Spooner Junction. A fee is charged for use of the park.

When other areas in the Lake Tahoe area are suffering from poor snow conditions, the snow along the Marlette Lake tour is usually better. Another good feature of this tour is that snowmobiles are prohibited in this area.

Marlette Lake was formed in the 1870s when a dam was built across Marlette Creek. The lake water was used in the mining area of Virginia City.

Begin the tour by skiing 0.7 miles to the spot where the North Canyon Creek tour (no. 53) intersects North Canyon Creek (**8**). Cross the creek and continue on the road, which heads up North Canyon and parallels the creek, for 2.5 miles to a large, open area (**10**) where you have a view to the south of the peaks which form the eastern boundary of Desolation Wilderness, including Mt. Tallac. Up to this open area, the tour is suitable for advancing beginner skiers. Beyond this point, the route is steeper, and the slopes you cross are potential avalanche paths.

From the open area, climb north on the road for 0.6 mile to the saddle (**11**) between Snow Valley Peak and Peak 8738. From the saddle, you can see Marlette Lake, to which you descend north on the road for 0.7 mile and 400′. You can also extend the tour by skiing on the road along the west shore of the lake to the dam.

56 Government Meadow

MAP 27
PAGE 131

Difficulty	1
Length	Short
Elevation	7000/Nil
Navigation	Adjacent to plowed road
Time	Short
Season	Mid-December through mid-April
USGS topo	15′ series, Fallen Leaf Lake
Start	From Highway 50 in Meyers, follow Highway 89 south for 4.3 miles. There will be a turnout on the east (left) side of the road.

Although the meadow is small and surrounded by trees, you can see it from the road on the east side, and adjacent to the parking area. This meadow is a good place to experience ski touring for the first time.

Cozy snow cave   *Kim Grandfield*

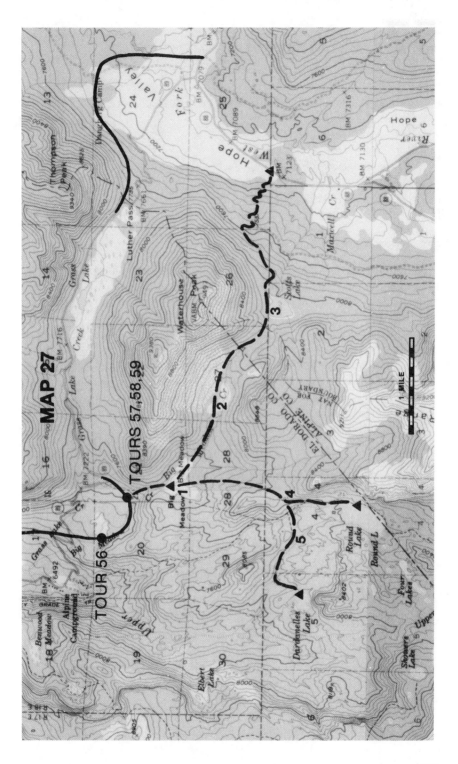

57 Big Meadow

MAP 27
PAGE 131

Difficulty	2
Length	1 mile round trip
Elevation	7300/ + 200, − 200
Navigation	Map
Time	Few hours
Season	December through April
USGS topo	15′ series, Fallen Leaf Lake, Freel Peak
Start	From Highway 50 in Meyers, follow Highway 89 south for exactly 5.0 miles. There will be a turnout on the north (left) side of the road.

Although the route itself to Big Meadow is not particularly interesting, the meadow and the surrounding area are pleasant to explore. Big Meadow is also a landmark on the Scotts Lake tour and the Round Lake and Dardanelles Lake tour.

Leave Highway 89 from the side of the road opposite the turnout where normally there is a heavily worn path leading south to Big Meadow. The trail is relatively steep, especially the first part, and it is easier to walk this section if the path is hard-packed. If no trail exists, ski south along the east (left) side of the creek which flows from Big Meadow and which crosses the road 50 yards downhill from the turnout. Stay far enough to the left to avoid the brush.

Winter camping

MAP 27
PAGE 131

Scotts Lake **58**

Difficulty	3
Length	6 miles round trip or 5 miles one-way to Hope Valley
Elevation	7300/+700, −700 round trip or 7300/+700, −900 one-way to Hope Valley
Navigation	Road and map
Time	Half day
Season	Mid-December through mid-April
USGS topo	15' series, Fallen Leaf Lake, Freel Peak
Start	From Highway 50 in Meyers, follow Highway 89 south for exactly 5.0 miles. There will be a turnout on the north (left) side of the road.
End	You can return to the starting point or end the tour on Highway 88 in Hope Valley. The ending point on Highway 88 is 1.5 miles southwest of the junction of Highways 88 and 89 (Picketts Junction). There is an old gate on the west side of the road.

This tour gives you the feeling of seclusion as you navigate through woods. It is a good choice for strong advancing beginner skiers who want to get away from the very easy-to-follow routes of most beginner tours. By making this tour a one-way trip to Hope Valley, you also have a wonderful downhill run, with lots of room to maneuver, from Scotts Lake to the valley.

Begin the tour by following the Big Meadow tour (no. 57) to Big Meadow (**1**). Turn southeast (left) and ski along the north (left) side of Big Meadow Creek until it enters the woods. Continue along the creek for 0.7 mile until you reach another meadow (**2**). Locate the road on the far north (left) side of it.

From the meadow, follow the road gradually uphill for 1.0 mile and then descend a short slope to Scotts Lake (**3**). To the north of the lake is Waterhouse Peak, to the east is Hope Valley, and the horizon to the east is dominated by Pickett and Hawkins Peaks.

To continue to Hope Valley, ski east on the road which passes on the north side of Scotts Lake and begin to descend to the valley and Highway 88. Because the road becomes steeper as you descend, you may want to leave the road and pick your own path to the east if you need more room. Feel free to zig-zag down through the fairly open woods where the telemarking terrain is excellent. If you encounter a road junction as you descend, take the fork which heads east until you reach Highway 88.

Difficulty	4
Length	5 miles round trip to Round Lake or 6 miles round trip to Dardanelles Lake
Elevation	7300/+1050, −1050 to Round Lake or 7300/+1250, −1250 to Dardanelles Lake
Navigation	Map and compass
Time	Full day
Season	Mid-December through mid-April
USGS topo	15′ series, Fallen Leaf Lake, Freel Peak
Start	From Highway 50 in Meyers, follow Highway 89 south for exactly 5.0 miles. There will be a turnout on the north (left) side of the road.

Since most tourers will not want the challenge of navigation by map and compass, you can expect to be alone once you leave Big Meadow.

Both Round Lake and Dardanelles Lake are located in the Upper Truckee River drainage. Of the two lakes, Round Lake is easier to find. Dardanelles Lake is more difficult to find because it is situated among trees in a rugged area.

Begin the tour by skiing to Big Meadow (1) as described in the Big Meadow tour (no. 57). Ski south across the meadow and then climb gradually south for 0.8 mile. As you climb, you parallel a creek on your east (left) side and traverse a ridge on your west (right) side. When you are 0.8 mile south of Big Meadow (there is no landmark), veer slightly west and climb for 0.2 mile to a saddle (4). To the west of the saddle is the Upper Truckee River drainage.

Round Lake. Round Lake is located 0.8 mile from the saddle. To reach the lake, descend the west side of the saddle by traversing to the south. Once you are down to more level terrain, continue to ski south and parallel to the steep cliffs and pass below a prominent rock outcropping until you reach the lake.

Dardanelles Lake. Descend 200′ directly down the west side of the saddle (4) until the terrain levels and you cross a creek. Immediately after crossing the creek, you may encounter another creek which you cross. If necessary, ski upstream to cross these creeks. Continue west through an open area, across a frozen pond and down to another creek (5). Descend along the northeast (right) side of the creek for 0.5 mile. Cross the creek and climb south for 0.3 mile to Dardanelles Lake. You should be aware that if you are forced to cross the last creek upstream of the described location, you will find the skiing on the southwest (side) much more difficult.

MAP 28
PAGE 136

Grass Lake 60

Difficulty	1
Length	Short
Elevation	7700/Nil
Navigation	Adjacent to plowed road
Time	Short
Season	December through April
USGS topo	15' series, Freel Peak
Start	Highway 89, anywhere from Luther Pass west for 1.5 miles.

Grass Lake and the meadow surrounding it form a 1.5-mile-long flat area along the south side of Highway 89. Close to South Lake Tahoe, this area is excellent for practicing ski touring techniques. Beginners can experience easy downhill runs on the slopes to the south. On the west end of the meadow, an old road which enters the trees can be followed for a short distance. Be aware that it may not be safe to ski on the lake.

Note the form!

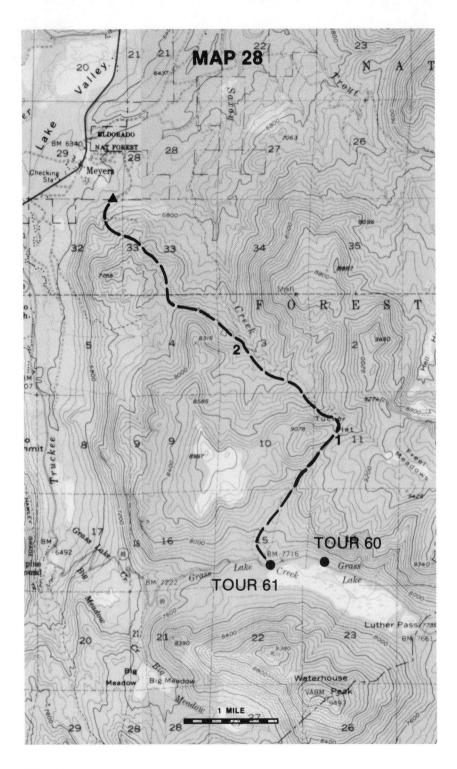

MAP 28

1 MILE

136

MAP 28
PAGE 136

Grass Lake to Meyers **61**

Difficulty	4
Length	6 miles one-way
Elevation	7700/+1100, −2300
Navigation	Map and compass
Time	Full day
Season	Late December through early April
USGS topo	15′ series, Freel Peak, Fallen Leaf Lake
Start	From Highway 50 in Meyers follow Highway 89 south for 6.8 miles to the first turnout, which borders a meadow and Grass Lake, on the south (right) side of the road.
End	Tahoe Paradise residential area near Meyers. From Highway 50, follow Apache Avenue into the residential area and find a parking place; Lost Lane is a good location. Dense woods near the end of the tour make it difficult to end the tour at a specific point so carry a local map of the Meyers area on the tour so that you can find your car.

The beauty of this route is that long after the snow has thawed and consolidated in other areas, this route normally still offers powder snow conditions in the upper reaches of Saxon Creek, which is, coincidentally, the location of the downhill run from Tucker Flat.

This tour also challenges advanced skiers—the terrain is steep, the navigation is critical, and the skiing in the dense woods is difficult.

From the north side of Highway 89 at the starting point, ski north and slightly west for 0.2 mile until you intersect a creek. Climb northeast and parallel to the creek at a steep angle for 1.5 miles to the saddle (1) between Peaks 9426 and 9078; only attempt this ascent when there is absolutely no avalanche danger. Tucker Flat is just to the northeast of the saddle.

From the saddle, descend northwest, paralleling but staying above the summer trail and Saxon Creek. The descent is steep, but, hopefully, covered with powder snow. Descend for 1.5 miles to an elevation of 7600′ (2); if you do not have an altimeter, you can estimate the correct elevation by carefully studying the topo.

At the 7600′ elevation point, turn away from Saxon Creek and the summer trail. Traverse northwest below Peak 8316 and maintain your elevation for 1.0 mile. Now traverse north for 0.5 mile and then descend northwest to the Tahoe Paradise residential area. Be aware that if you drop down too early, you end up in an undergrowth where it is impossible to ski.

Road makes the navigation easy

Echo Summit

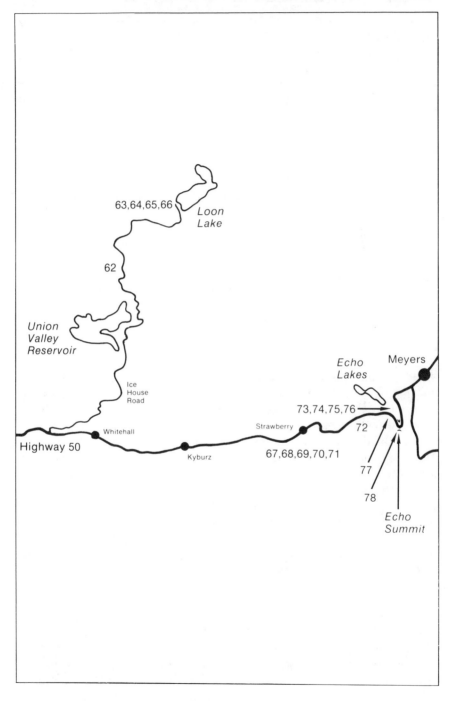

63,64,65,66 Loon
Lake

62

Union
Valley
Reservoir

Ice
House
Road

Echo   Meyers
Lakes

73,74,75,76

Strawberry   72

Highway 50   Whitehall

Kyburz   67,68,69,70,71

77

78

Echo
Summit

Difficulty	3
Length	5 miles round trip via short route, 9 miles round trip via long route or 8 miles via the loop
Elevation	5600/+1100, -1100 via short route, 5450/+1250, -1250 via long route or 5600/+1250, -1250 via the loop
Navigation	Road and map
Time	Half day to most of a day
Season	January through March
USGS topo	15' series, Robbs Peak; 7.5' series, Robbs Peak
Start	From Highway 50 turn north onto Ice House Road and drive for 21 miles until you reach to a saddle. Continue for 0.8 mile until you reach a snow-covered road on the west (left) side of Ice House Road which marks the starting point of the "short route." The "long route" starts 1.2 miles ahead on the west (left) side of Ice House Road at the snow-covered road which heads to Uncle Toms Cabin. The road to Uncle Toms Cabin is located 100 yards before the turnoff to South Fork Campground.

The presence of a fire lookout, although abandoned, atop Robbs Peak attests to a commanding view. As you enjoy a leisurely lunch at the summit, look east to the impressive Crystal Range. After lunch, you can practice your telemark turns on the gradual slopes near the summit.

You can reach Robbs Peak by either of two routes which follow roads. These two routes combined with an additional 1.2 miles make an excellent loop trip.

Short route. On the west side of Ice House Road at the starting point is a very large clearing. The short route makes a loop to the north and then south through this clearing. Because the road is almost impossible to follow in this area, try climbing directly west and up the clearing toward the trees. As you near the trees, you can locate the road running north-south and parallel to the trees.

After locating the road, ski south on it for 1.4 miles to a distinctive saddle (1) located to the south of Robbs Peak. From the saddle, continue north on the road for 0.6 mile to the lookout atop Robbs Peak. The road traverses along the east side of the south ridge of Robbs Peak and leads to the open slopes of the summit.

Long route. Climb very gradually to the west for 2.3 miles on the snow-covered road which heads to Uncle Toms Cabin until you reach a saddle

(2). At the saddle, locate the junction between the road you are on and an obvious road which gradually descends to the south. At this road junction, there is also an obscure road which climbs southeast along a ridge. Follow this road and the ridge to the southeast for 2.1 miles to the summit of Robbs Peak.

Loop. The ideal way to visit Robbs Peak is to make a loop by ascending via the short route and descending via the long route.

When you have returned to the starting point of the long route, ski south on the west side of and parallel to Ice House Road for 1.2 miles and 150′ of elevation gain until you reach the starting point of the short route.

There is an abandoned road which you can follow for part of this distance.

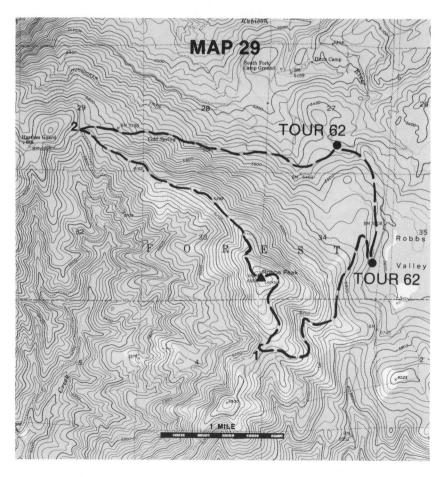

Helicopter skiing!

MAP **30**
PAGE 145

Berts Lake and Peak 6836 **63**

Difficulty	3
Length	2 miles round trip
Elevation	6400/+400, −400
Navigation	Marked trail and map
Time	Few hours
Season	Late December through early April
USGS topo	15' series, Robbs Peak; 7.5' series, Loon Lake
Start	Near Loon Lake on Ice House Road. From Highway 50 turn north onto Ice House Road. Drive 24 miles and in order to stay on Ice House Road, turn right. Continue for 5.4 miles until you reach the powerhouse building on the east (right) side of the road. Continue for another 100 yards to a parking area on the west (left) side of the road.

This very short tour to Berts Lake and Peak 6836 is an excellent choice for skiers who want to experience a tour of intermediate difficulty for the first time. The views from the lake and the peak make this excursion well worth the effort. At the parking area, locate the SMUD rain gauge and the markers which lead south. Follow the markers as best you can. If you lose them, continue to ski south and up towards the ridge top. Your goal is to reach the level section of the ridge top (**1**) to the north of Peak 6836.

From the level spot on the ridge, continue south and around the east side of Peak 6836. After you pass the peak, continue to traverse to the west along its south side until you see a saddle. Ski to the saddle where you find Berts Lake.

From the saddle, you can climb 100' to the northeast to the summit of Peak 6836. From Berts Lake, you can return to the starting point by re-tracing your route or by descending to the west until you intersect the Chipmunk Bluff tour which you can follow back to the starting point.

64 Chipmunk Bluff

MAP 30
PAGE 145

Difficulty	2
Length	3 miles round trip
Elevation	6400/+450, −450
Navigation	Road
Time	Half day
Season	Late December through early April
USGS topo	15′ series, Robbs Peak; 7.5′ series, Loon Lake
Start	Near Loon Lake on Ice House Road. From Highway 50 turn north onto Ice House Road. Drive 24 miles and in order to stay on Ice House Road, turn right. Continue for 5.4 miles until you reach the powerhouse building on the east (right) side of the road. Continue for another 100 yards to a parking area on the west (left) side of the road.

This pleasant tour on a road is ideal for skiers seeking a short, easy tour. From the Chipmunk Bluff vicinity, there are good views to enjoy while having lunch. Be aware that the last 75 vertical feet to the summit of Chipmunk Bluff are not skiable and are dangerous to climb due to its precipitous angle and the presence of cornices at the top.

From the parking area, descend to the southwest on the road for a short distance. Start to climb and follow the road as it turns south. You will pass under power lines 0.5 mile from the starting point and you continue on the road for 0.2 mile to a saddle (2).

From the saddle, descend south on the road for 0.4 mile until you reach a level section of road. Ahead climb gradually on the road for 0.1 until it disappears. Continue to climb gradually southwest for 0.2 mile to the base of the very steep section which leads to the summit of Chipmunk Bluff.

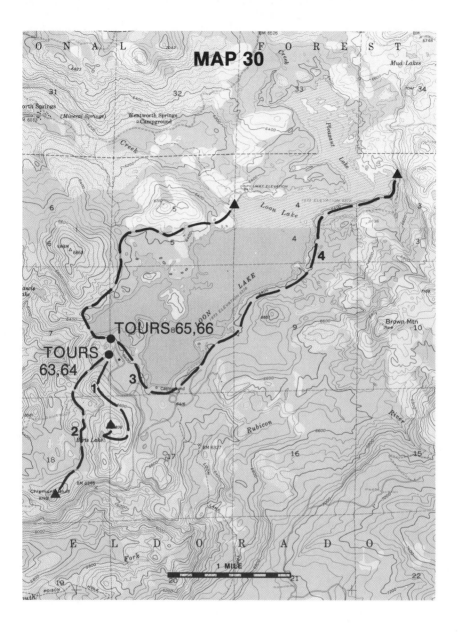

MAP 30

South Shore of Loon Lake

Difficulty	1–2
Length	Up to 7 miles round trip
Elevation	6400/Nil
Navigation	Adjacent to plowed road and map
Time	Up to most of a day
Season	Late December through early April
USGS topo	15′ series, Robbs Peak, Granite Chief; 7.5′ series, Loon Lake, Wentworth Springs
Start	End of the plowed road at Loon Lake. From Highway 50 turn north onto Ice House Road. Drive 24 miles and in order to stay on Ice House Road, turn right. Continue for 5.4 miles until you reach the powerhouse building on the east (right) side of the road. Continue for 100 yards until you pass a parking area on the west (left) side of the road and then another 100 yards to the end of the plowed road.

Although this tour is not very difficult, skiers of all abilities can enjoy the unusual beauty of Loon Lake. The stark setting created by the vast lake basin, surrounding granite peaks, and sparse greenery may make you feel like you are on the moon.

From the plowed road, ski down to the edge of and then south along the lake. You will encounter a powerhouse building **(3)** (not the one by the road) just before reaching the south end of the lake. Ski up and around this building and continue to the south end of the lake. Due to fluctuating water levels, the ice on Loon Lake is unstable and dangerous. So, stay off the lake.

Continue to ski along the lake to the northeast as far as you desire. The terrain is filled with very gradual slopes and small rock outcroppings around which to weave. When you reach the building at Deer Crossing Camp **(4)**, you are 2.5 miles from the starting point.

After you pass Deer Crossing Camp, the skiing becomes slightly more difficult. From the camp, ski along Loon Lake and then along Pleasant Lake for 1.0 mile to a tunnel in the cliff. This tunnel connects Buck Island Lake Reservoir with Pleasant Lake. The tunnel is the farthest point of this tour.

If you wish to continue to the North Shore of Loon Lake tour, ski around the north end of Pleasant Lake where you can expect to negotiate many small obstacles, the most difficult of which is the creek formed by water exiting the tunnel. When you are 1.0 mile northeast of the northern dam of Loon Lake (the destination of the North Shore of Loon Lake tour), expect to cross or ski around several small ridges and gullies. The distance of the loop around Loon and Pleasant Lakes is 7.0 miles.

Cody Hut

66 North Shore of Loon Lake

MAP 30
PAGE 145

Difficulty	1
Length	Up to 4 miles round trip
Elevation	6400/Nil
Navigation	Road
Time	Up to half day
Season	Late December through early April
USGS topo	15' series, Robbs Peak, Granite Chief; 7.5' series, Loon Lake, Wentworth Springs
Start	End of the plowed road at Loon Lake. From Highway 50 turn north onto Ice House Road. Drive 24 miles and in order to stay on Ice House Road, turn right. Continue for 5.4 miles until you reach the powerhouse building on the east (right) side of the road. Continue for 100 yards until you pass a parking area on the west (left) side of the road and then another 100 yards to the end of the plowed road.

The tour along the north shore of Loon Lake is the easiest tour in this area and offers beginners an opportunity to experience skiing in this stark, yet beautiful, basin.

From the starting point, ski northwest on the snow-covered road for 0.1 mile to the southern dam which you cross. Continue on the road for 1.6 miles to the northern dam which is the destination of this tour.

If you prefer to avoid the road but want an easy tour, consider the South Shore of Loon Lake tour. Its description also provides information about skiing around Loon and Pleasant Lakes.

MAP 31
PAGE 152

Strawberry Canyon Road 67

Difficulty	2–3
Length	Up to 9 miles round trip
Elevation	5600/Up to +1100, −1100
Navigation	Road
Time	Up to full day
Season	Late December through early April
USGS topo	15' series, Fallen Leaf Lake; 7.5' series, Pyramid Peak, Echo Lake
Start	42-Mile Recreation Site on Highway 50, 0.5 mile southwest of Strawberry.

The best reason for choosing to ski in the uncrowded 42-Mile Recreation Site area is its proximity to Sacramento and the Bay Area. Of all the tours beginning at the site trailhead, Strawberry Canyon Road, which parallels the north side of Strawberry Creek, is used the least. Since this tour has no particular destination, you can tailor the length to your desires. The track you make while climbing very gradually up the road makes for an excellent glide on your return.

At the starting point, cross the bridge to the southeast side of the South Fork of the American River and immediately turn south (right) toward Strawberry Creek Tract. Ski 0.6 mile on the road to the junction of Strawberry Canyon and Cody Summit Roads (1). In that first section, stay on the obvious main road and ignore the small roads which lead into the cabin areas.

At the junction, turn north (left) and ski on Strawberry Canyon Road for 0.2 mile until you pass a small road on your left where the main road turns southeast. Continue as far as you desire on Strawberry Canyon Road and then turn around.

From the junction with the small road on your left, continuing on the road for 1.5 miles brings you to an impressive, awe-inspiring avalanche chute (2) created in the winter of 1983. That season's record snowfall left a huge snowpack on this steep slope. When warm weather followed, the melted snow saturated the decomposed granite to form a quicksand-like mass. Even the dense stand of large, mature trees could not hold back the weight of this mass.

From the avalanche site on the road, you reach a gate (3) in 1.5 miles and you reach Strawberry Creek in another 0.7 mile. Strawberry Creek is 4.5 miles from the starting point, and intermediate skiers can cross the creek and follow an obscure road still farther up Strawberry Canyon.

68 Strawberry Ridge Loop

MAP 31
PAGE 152

Difficulty	3
Length	5 miles round trip
Elevation	5600/+1150, −1150
Navigation	Road and marked trail
Time	Half day
Season	Late December through early April
USGS topo	15' series, Fallen Leaf Lake; 7.5' series, Pyramid Peak
Start	42-Mile Recreation Site on Highway 50, 0.5 mile southwest of Strawberry.

The highlight of this tour is having lunch on the ridge above Strawberry Canyon. Along the route you will find an assortment of wide and narrow roads, and mild and steep slopes.

At the starting point, cross the bridge to the southeast side of the South Fork of the American River and immediately turn south (right) toward Strawberry Creek Tract. Follow the road for 0.6 mile, ignoring the small roads which lead into the cabin areas, to the junction of Strawberry Canyon and Cody Summit Roads (1).

At the junction, continue on the fork to the southeast (right) for 0.2 mile until you reach the bridge at Strawberry Creek (4). Immediately after crossing the creek, turn southeast (left) at the road junction onto the road which parallels the creek.

From the junction, ski 0.1 mile until you pass a road on your right (5). You will be returning to this point on the road you have just passed. Continue on the road you have been on for 0.5 mile to a junction (6) where you take the south (right) fork. Past this junction, the route climbs at a much steeper angle.

Continue on the road for 0.5 mile until you make a 180 degree right turn with the road. Continue for 0.3 mile until you make a 180 degree left turn with the road. Ski 100 yards past the last turn and locate the marker which indicates where the route leaves the main road (7).

From the main road, take the marked trail which follows an obscure road and climbs southwest for 0.5 mile to the ridge top (8). If, after reaching the ridge top, you still want to climb, you can explore the ridge to the southeast for 0.7 mile before resuming the tour.

From the ridge, descend to the southwest for 0.2 mile until you intersect a jeep road. Follow the jeep road as it gradually turns north for 0.3 mile until it starts to turn east. When the road begins to turn east, leave it and descend to the northwest down a clearing for about 75 yards until you intersect another jeep trail and the Cody Creek Loop (9).

Continue north on the merged trails (an obscure road) for 0.3 mile until you cross a ridge. Ski another 0.1 mile until the jeep trail becomes a regular road. Finally, ski east for 0.2 mile to the junction **(5)** with the road you skied earlier. At the junction, turn northwest and retrace your tracks to the starting point.

Packsaddle Pass area

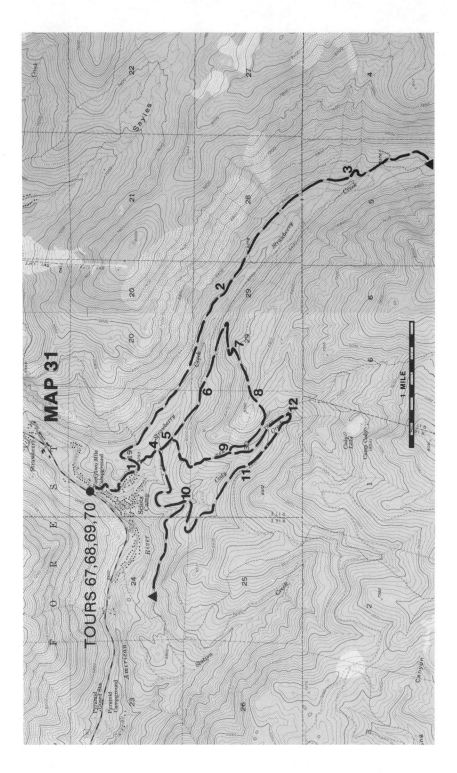

MAP 31

TOURS 67, 68, 69, 70

152

MAP 31
PAGE 152

Station Creek Trail **69**

Difficulty	2
Length	5 miles round trip
Elevation	5600/ + 550, − 550
Navigation	Road
Time	Up to half day
Season	Late December through early April
USGS topo	15′ series, Fallen Leaf Lake; 7.5′ series, Pyramid Peak
Start	42-Mile Recreation Site on Highway 50, 0.5 mile southwest of Strawberry.

This tour takes you on easy-to-follow and gradually sloping roads to a beautiful view of the South Fork of the American River Canyon, the sheer rock face of Lovers Leap, and Ralston Peak. Start this tour by following the Strawberry Ridge Loop tour (no. 68) for 0.8 mile to Strawberry Creek **(4)**. Cross the creek on the bridge and immediately encounter a road junction. Continue on the road to the west (right) for 0.7 mile to another road junction **(10)**.

At this junction, take the fork to the northwest (right) and descend gradually for 0.8 mile until you reach an excellent view to the northeast. At this point, you are 2.3 miles from the starting point. This vantage point is the destination of the tour although the road and a marked ski touring trail do continue.

70 Cody Creek Loop

MAP 31
PAGE 152

Difficulty	3
Length	5 miles round trip
Elevation	5600/+900, −900
Navigation	Road
Time	Half day
Season	Late December through early April
USGS topo	15′ series, Fallen Leaf Lake; 7.5′ series, Pyramid Peak
Start	42-Mile Recreation Site on Highway 50, 0.5 mile southwest of Strawberry.

This tour follows a road which climbs very gradually until it heads up Cody Creek and becomes steeper as the canyon closes in. If you are just progressing into intermediate touring, note that this loop is slightly easier than the nearby Strawberry Ridge Loop.

Begin by following the Strawberry Ridge Loop tour (no. 68) for 0.8 mile to Strawberry Creek (**4**). Immediately after crossing the bridge, you encounter a road junction. Continue on the road heading west (right) for 0.7 mile until you pass the Station Creek Trail turnoff (**10**) on your right. Continue on the main road for 100 yards to another junction.

At the junction, follow the road to the west (right) for 0.3 mile until you make a 180 degree left turn with the road. Continue on the road for 0.7 mile until you pass a road on your right (**11**) which leads to Packsaddle Pass.

Continue straight on the road for 0.6 mile until it crosses Cody Creek (**12**). Immediately after crossing the creek, follow a small road as it descends along the creek for 0.6 mile to a point where this tour merges with the Strawberry Ridge Loop tour (**9**).

Continue north on the merged trails (an obscure road) for 0.3 mile until you cross a small ridge. Continue for 0.1 mile until the road becomes more distinct. Continue following this road east for 0.2 mile to a junction (**5**). Turn northwest (left) and ski 0.1 mile to the bridge across Strawberry Creek where you retrace your tracks to your car.

Becker Peak

71 Packsaddle Pass

MAP 32
PAGE 157

Difficulty	3
Length	10 miles round trip
Elevation	5600/ + 1550, − 1550
Navigation	Road
Time	Full day
Season	Late December through early April
USGS topo	15′ series, Fallen Leaf Lake; 7.5′ series, Pyramid Peak
Start	42-Mile Recreation Site on Highway 50, 0.5 mile southwest of Strawberry.

You reach Packsaddle Pass, where spectacular views of the smooth, tapering profile of Pyramid Peak and the Crystal Range await you, by a long, gradual climb on a wide road. Expect the views to be obscured by trees until you are 0.8 mile from the summit.

The last 0.8 mile ends at the edge of a wide, open plateau, an inviting sample of the excellent ski touring terrain in this area. Unfortunately, the half-day or so you spend climbing to reach this area leaves you with little time to further explore. If you want to spend more time in this area, consider staying a couple of nights at the ski hut in Cody Meadows. The hut is operated by Fred Hartmeyer whom you can contact at:

> Cody Hut Ski Treks
> 3250 Forni Road
> Placerville, California 95667

At the starting point, cross the bridge to the southeast side of the South Fork of the American River and immediately turn south (right) toward Strawberry Creek Tract. Follow the road for 0.6 mile, ignoring the small roads which lead into the cabin areas, to the junction of Strawberry Canyon and Cody Summit Roads (1).

At the junction, continue on the fork to the southeast (right) for 0.2 mile until you reach the bridge at Strawberry Creek (2). Immediately after crossing the bridge, you encounter a fork in the road. Take the fork to the west (right) and ski for 0.7 mile until you pass a road on your right (3). Ski another 100 yards until you pass a road on your left.

Continue on the main road for 1.0 mile until you reach a road junction (4). At the junction, take the road which turns west (right) and follow it for 1.5 miles to another road junction (5). You now follow the fork to the west (right) for 1.2 miles to Packsaddle Pass.

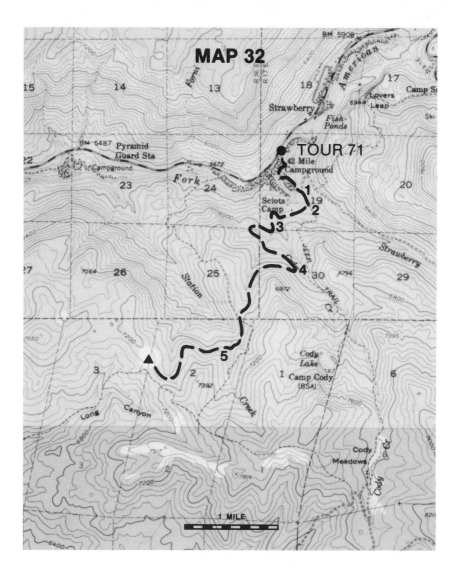

MAP 32

TOUR 71

MAP 33
PAGE 159

72 Sayles Canyon

Difficulty	4
Length	9 miles one-way
Elevation	7150/ + 1950, − 2600
Navigation	Road, map and compass
Time	Full day
Season	Late December through mid-April
USGS topo	15′ series, Fallen Leaf Lake; 7.5′ series, Echo Lake
Start	Highway 50, 1.2 miles east of the turnoff to Sierra Ski Ranch and 2.0 miles west of Echo Summit Maintenance Station. On the south side of the highway there is a snow-covered road and a small little building raised off the ground on poles.
End	Sayles Canyon Tract, 0.4 mile east of Camp Sacramento.

The following synopsis will surely entice advanced skiers to this tour: In the first 1.6 miles you climb 1300′ to a ridge which overlooks the Upper Truckee River and has views of Lake Tahoe. For the next 1.9 miles the route rolls along perfect ski touring terrain to the highest point of the tour. Ahead of you is a 5.3 mile descent of 2400′. You are guaranteed of solitude, fine views, and a route-finding challenge if you choose this tour.

Begin the tour by following the snow-covered road on the south side of the highway for 0.3 mile to the edge of a meadow (1). From the meadow's edge, leave the road and climb at a very steep angle to the southeast for 1.3 miles to the microwave station on the ridge top (2). Although you may cross some Sno-Cat tracks as you climb, the best route is to head straight up. When you reach the microwave station, congratulate yourself for having completed the most significant climbing, relax, and enjoy the views.

From the microwave station, ski south along the ridge for 0.4 mile to the huge microwave tower (3) at the end of the aerial tramway. Continue skiing to the southwest on the ridge for 0.7 mile and then turn south onto a ridge which you follow for 0.8 mile to the summit of Peak 8905 (4).

From Peak 8905, descend through an open area to the south for 0.1 mile until you enter very dense trees. Pick your way south through the trees for 0.2 mile to a broad saddle (5). Now ski southwest for another 0.1 mile to the edge of Bryan Meadow.

From Bryan Meadow, descend through the trees to the southwest for 1.0 mile to a clearing (6). You now follow Sayles Canyon to the northwest for 2.2 miles of gradual downhill. Expect a pleasant downhill run where you weave through the trees by making quick slalom turns.

After 2.2 miles of gradual terrain, the terrain becomes noticeably steeper, and you must assess the conditions to determine on which side of the creek to continue your descent. Keep in mind that you eventually want to be on the east (right) side. Descend the steep section for 1.0 mile until you encounter a road **(7)** on the east side of the creek. Follow this road to the north for 0.5 mile to the end of the tour.

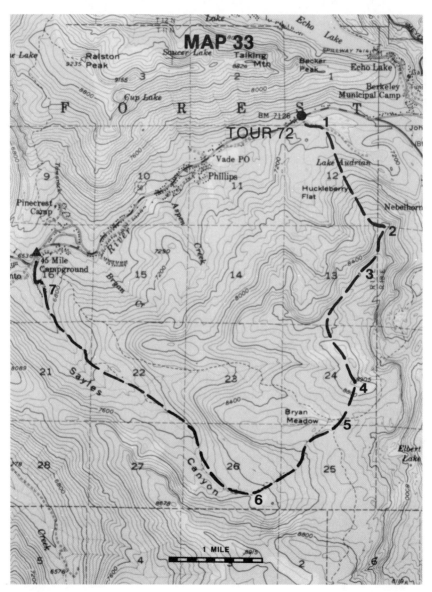

73 Becker Peak

MAP 34
PAGE 161

Difficulty	3
Length	4 miles round trip
Elevation	7350/ + 1000, − 1000
Navigation	Road and map
Time	Few hours
Season	Mid-December through mid-April
USGS topo	15′ series, Fallen Leaf Lake; 7.5′ series, Echo Lake
Start	From 1.2 miles west of Echo Summit Maintenance Station and 0.2 mile west of Little Norway on Highway 50, drive 0.6 mile east towards Berkeley Camp until you reach the unplowed road which leads to Echo Lakes.

The Becker Peak tour is the most rewarding short tour in the Echo Summit area. The route along a ridge offers excellent ski touring terrain and magnificent views of Lake Tahoe, Echo Lakes, Talking Mountain, and the mountains to the south. Because this route is so enjoyable, don't feel compelled to reach the summit, the ascent of which can be tricky and dangerous.

From the starting point, ski north for 0.4 mile on the snow-covered road toward Echo Lake. When you have gone 0.4 mile (there is no landmark), leave the road and climb northwest to the ridge (1) of which Becker Peak is a part. If you pass the turnoff point, ski until the road begins to descend. At this point, you can climb southwest at a very steep angle for 0.2 mile to get on the ridge.

Once on the ridge, ski west along it until you reach a small high point (2) which juts up from the ridge; ahead is the crux of the tour. Up to this point, you will find the ridge broad and gently sloped except for a short, narrow section which is passable without much difficulty. All along the ridge, be sure to stay away from the steep northern edges. Along this first section, there are many spots where you can stop to relax and enjoy the fine views. You should be aware of possible avalanche conditions and ice if you choose to proceed past the crux point.

To proceed, climb toward the high point. At an appropriate point (there is no landmark), traverse around its south side to its west side. From the west side of the high point, climb the last steep but straightforward 250′ to the summit of Becker Peak.

You actually approach the summit from the south, and the last 50 vertical feet over rocks may be dangerous due to icy conditions.

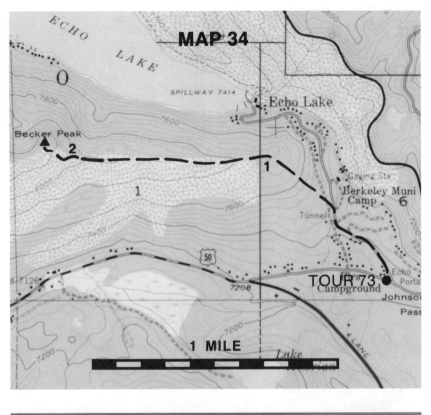

MAP 34

ECHO LAKE

SPILLWAY 7414

Echo Lake

Becker Peak

2

1

Gaging Sta

Berkeley Muni
Camp

6

Tunnel

50

TOUR 73

Echo
Porta

Campground

Johnsor

Pass

7126

7208

1 MILE

7200

Lake

LANE

Echo Lakes   *Gary Clark*

Snow sculpture   *Bob Bastasz*

MAP 35
PAGE 165

Echo Lakes 74

Difficulty	2
Length	2 to 6 miles round trip
Elevation	7350/ + 250, − 250
Navigation	Road
Time	Few hours to half day
Season	January through March
USGS topo	15′ series, Fallen Leaf Lake
Start	From 1.2 miles west of Echo Summit Maintenance Station and 0.2 mile west of Little Norway on Highway 50, drive 0.6 mile east towards Berkeley Camp until you reach the unplowed road which leads to Echo Lakes.

With lots of room to ski, the Echo Lakes area is a popular and beautiful destination. The lakes are a perfect place for a leisurely day or night tour; by moonlight, the skiing seems effortless along the glowing lakes. You can even enjoy yourself at Echo Lakes during stormy, windy weather. Two people holding a jacket between them, or even better a small tarp, can literally sail across the hard surface at amazingly high speeds. Echo Lakes is also a great place to fly a kite if you have a durable one and unbreakable string.

Echo Lakes are usually solid enough to safely ski on during the months of January, February and March. Regardless of the month, you should always assess the conditions before skiing on the lakes.

To insure the good reputation of cross-country skiers, please respect the many privately owned cabins at Echo Lakes. Also, be aware that overnight camping is not permissible there. If you are interested in an overnight tour in this area you can ski all or part of the way to Desolation Valley as described separately in this guidebook.

From the starting point, ski north for 1.1 miles on the snow-covered road. In this section, you can expect a gradual climb followed by a short but steep descent to Lower Echo Lake. If it is safe, ski northwest across the lower lake.

From the northwest end of the lower lake, ski 0.1 mile farther to Upper Echo Lake. After reaching the upper lake, you can continue northwest to its end.

If Echo Lakes are not safe to ski on, you can ski along the edge where the summer trail skirts them. Unfortunately, the slow and more difficult skiing along the trail is no substitute for the open, hard-packed surface of the lakes.

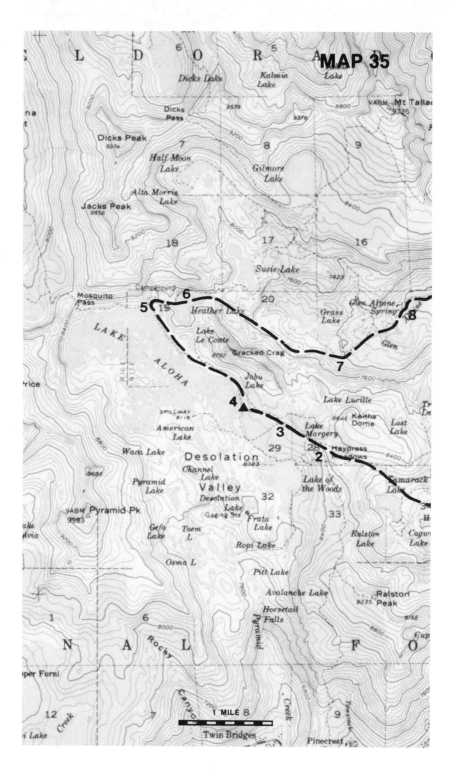

MAP 35

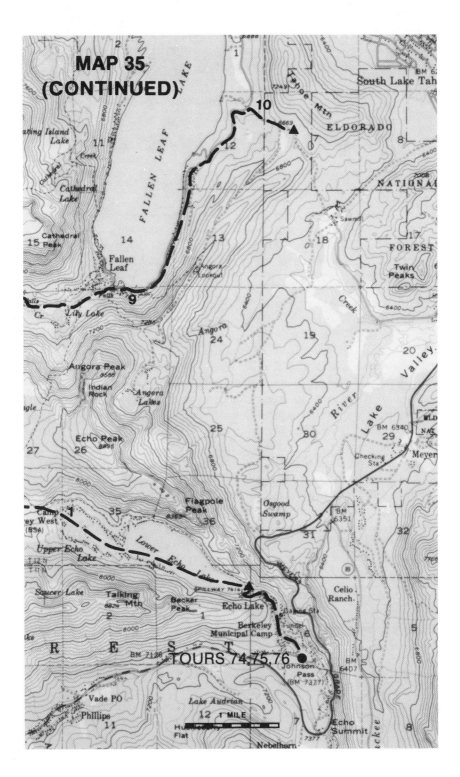

MAP 35
(CONTINUED)

TOURS 74,75,76

75 Desolation Valley

MAP 35
PAGES 164–165

Difficulty	3
Length	12 miles round trip
Elevation	7350/ + 1400, − 1400
Navigation	Road, map and compass
Time	Full day
Season	January through March
USGS topo	15′ series, Fallen Leaf Lake
Start	From 1.2 miles west of Echo Summit Maintenance Station and 0.2 mile west of Little Norway on Highway 50, drive 0.6 mile east towards Berkeley Camp until you reach the unplowed road which leads to Echo Lakes.

During winter, you can experience solitude in spectacular Desolation Valley without the crowd of summer backpackers. As you make your final descent to Lake Aloha, you are struck by the large, stark valley, the Crystal Range, and the smooth profile of Pyramid Peak. If you are planning a one-day trip to this area, expect to get only a glimpse of its beauty. To fully enjoy the valley's magnificence, plan a multi-day trip instead.

The tour to Desolation Valley covers a variety of terrain and is a challenging trip. The first part of this tour is across the very popular Echo Lakes; however, when you leave the lakes behind, you also leave most of the skiers behind.

Start the tour by skiing to the northwest end of Upper Echo Lake (1) as described in the Echo Lakes tour (no. 74). From the end of the lake, climb steadily northwest for 1.8 miles to Haypress Meadows (2).

From the meadow, continue northwest for 0.5 mile to the level area (3) west of Lake Margery. For the best route in this section, pass to the west of the lake. From the level area, descend west for 0.5 mile to the shore of Lake Aloha. You have now reached the heart of Desolation Valley.

Remains of igloo

76 Echo Summit to Fallen Leaf Lake

MAP 35
PAGES 164–165

Difficulty	5
Length	16 miles one-way
Elevation	7350/+1400, −2000
Navigation	Road, map and compass
Time	One very long day or two days
Season	January through March
USGS topo	15′ series, Fallen Leaf Lake
Start	From 1.2 miles west of Echo Summit Maintenance Station and 0.2 mile west of Little Norway on Highway 50, drive 0.6 mile east towards Berkeley Camp until you reach the unplowed road which leads to Echo Lakes.
End	From the intersection of Highways 50 and 89 in South Lake Tahoe, drive southwest on Lake Tahoe Blvd. for 2.7 miles and turn right onto Tahoe Mountain Road. Drive 1.1 miles and turn right onto Glenmore Way and then immediately left onto Dundee Circle. In 0.1 mile turn left onto Tahoe Mountain Road once again and park. Do not drive down the narrow plowed portion of Tahoe Mountain Road which is just ahead.

Pyramid Peak and the Crystal Range are among the impressive sights along this extremely long and remote tour. This tour is too difficult for most skiers to complete in one day, especially early in the season when daylight is in short supply. If you enjoy snowcamping, you may make this tour into a two-day trip by spending the night somewhere along Lake Aloha.

Start the tour by skiing to Lake Aloha (4) as described in the Desolation Valley tour (no. 75). After you reach the lake, ski northwest for 1.5 miles to the north shore where it rises abruptly to Jacks Peak. To the east of this steep rise is an obvious notch (5) through which you descend to Heather Lake (6). Exercise caution in the vicinity of Jacks Peak and on both sides of the ridge of which Cracked Crag is dominant since these slopes are subject to avalanche.

From Heather Lake, follow the outlet creek for 0.6 mile to the southeast until the creek turns north. Continue to ski southeast, paralleling Cracked Crag and the ridge, to a point (7) south of Grass Lake. From south of Grass Lake, descend northeast to Glen Alpine Spring (8) where you find a cabin and a road. When the snow depth is low, you should expect a difficult 0.9 mile from Grass Lake to Glen Alpine Spring due to brush and boulders.

From Glen Alpine Spring, descend on the road to Fallen Leaf Lake (9).

Ski on the road along the east side of the lake for 2.7 miles to the junction with Tahoe Mountain Road **(10)**. Turn east (right) onto Tahoe Mountain Road and ski 0.5 mile until the road is plowed. Walk 0.1 mile up the plowed road to Dundee Circle where the tour ends. You can also end this tour on Highway 89 by continuing along the east shore of Fallen Leaf Lake.

Desolation Valley *Gary Clark*

77 Lake Audrian

MAP 36
PAGE 171

Difficulty	3
Length	2 miles round trip
Elevation	7200/ + 100, − 100
Navigation	Road
Time	Few hours
Season	Mid-December through mid-April
USGS topo	15′ series, Fallen Leaf Lake; 7.5′ series, Echo Lake
Start	Little Norway on Highway 50, 1.0 mile west of Echo Summit Maintenance Station. The tour begins on the south side of the highway 50 yards east of Little Norway.

Years ago, Echo Nordic at Little Norway marked this route on which a few skiers would travel each weekend. Now that the center has closed shop and the tour to the lake has almost been forgotten, you can be assured of solitude.

From the highway, follow a road marked by yellow diamonds to the southwest for 0.5 mile to the creek (1) which drains the lake. From here the road continues west; however, you want to turn east (left) and follow the creek and blue diamond markers for 0.3 mile to the lake.

Group tour

MAP **36**
PAGE 171

Benwood Meadow **78**

Difficulty	2
Length	2 miles round trip
Elevation	7400/+100, −100
Navigation	Road and map
Time	Few hours
Season	Mid-December through mid-April
USGS topo	15′ series, Fallen Leaf Lake
Start	Echo Summit Maintenance Station on Highway 50.

This short, easy tour to a secluded meadow in the Echo Summit area is perfect for beginners. Locate the snow-covered road across the highway from the maintenance station. Ski south on this road for 0.3 mile until it ends in the Summer Home Tract. Just east of the road is a rim overlooking the Upper Truckee River and to the north you can see the south end of Lake Tahoe.

From the end of the road, continue south for 0.2 mile over level terrain strewn with boulders to a small lake. Continue skiing southwest for 0.4 mile into a bowl where Benwood Meadow is located.

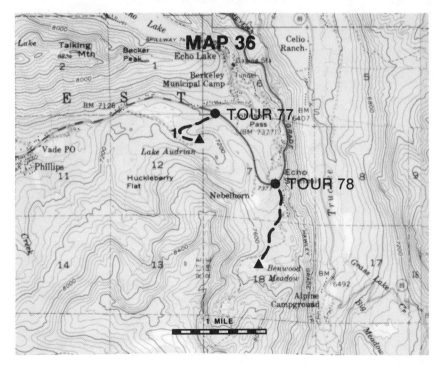

Wax of the day: pine tar, purple and grass

Nordic Ski Centers

The nordic centers listed here provide ski touring services and facilities, and are a good source for current snow, weather and avalanche conditions.

EAGLE MOUNTAIN NORDIC

Location	South of Highway 80 at the Yuba Gap exit.
Address	P.O. Box 89, Emigrant Gap, CA 95715
Phone	916-389-2254
Elevation	5750'

ROYAL GORGE CROSS COUNTRY SKI RESORT

Location	East of Highway 80 on Donner Pass Road at Soda Springs.
Address	P.O. Box 178, Soda Springs, CA 95728
Phone	916-426-3871
Elevation	7000'

CLAIR TAPPAAN LODGE

Location	East of Highway 80 on Donner Pass Road at Norden.
Address	P.O. Box 36, Norden, CA 95724
Phone	916-426-3632
Elevation	7000'

RONDI THORWALDSEN SKI TOURING CENTER

Location	North of Truckee in Tahoe Donner behind the Northwoods Clubhouse.
Address	P.O. Box 2462, Truckee, CA 95734
Phone	916-587-9821
Elevation	6600'

BIG CHIEF GUIDES

Location	On Highway 89 midway between Tahoe City and Truckee.
Address	P.O. Drawer AE, Truckee, CA 95734
Phone	916-587-4723
Elevation	6000'

SQUAW VALLEY NORDIC CENTER

Location	Old Papoose Ski Area in Squaw Valley off Highway 89 between Tahoe City and Truckee.
Address	P.O. Box 2637, Olympic Valley, CA 95730
Phone	916-583-8951
Elevation	6200'

TAHOE NORDIC SKI CENTER

Location	Two miles east of Tahoe City on Highway 28 and four blocks behind the Dollar Hill Shell Station.
Address	P.O. Box 1632, Tahoe City, CA 95730
Phone	916-583-9858
Elevation	6600'

NORTHSTAR NORDIC CENTER

Location	Off Highway 267 at Northstar Ski Resort.
Address	P.O. Box 129, Truckee, CA 95734
Phone	916-562-1010
Elevation	6400'

INCLINE CROSS-COUNTRY CENTER

Location	Incline's Executive Golf Course off Highway 431 in Incline Village.
Address	P.O. Box BN, Incline Village, NV 89450
Phone	702-831-5190
Elevation	6500'

ASCHI SPORTS CROSS COUNTRY

Location	In South Lake Tahoe at 3339 Lake Tahoe Blvd. (across the street from the main Bank of America).
Address	P.O. Box 16549, South Lake Tahoe, CA 95706
Phone	916-544-7873
Elevation	6200'

TELEMARK COUNTRY SPORTS

Location	On Highway 50 at Tahoe Paradise Golf Course near Meyers.
Address	P.O. Box 11975, Tahoe Paradise, CA 95708
Phone	916-577-6811
Elevation	6400'

ECHO SUMMIT NORDIC CENTER

Location   On Highway 50 at Echo Summit.
Address   P.O. Box 8955, South Lake Tahoe, CA
            95731
Phone   916-659-7154
Elevation   7400′

Pyramid Peak   *Gary Clark*